Executive Summary

In view of the ongoing severe abuses of religious freedom and based on the Iraqi government's toleration of these abuses as described in this report, particularly abuses against all of Iraq's most vulnerable and smallest religious minorities, the Commission recommends that Iraq should be designated a "country of particular concern" (CPC) under the International Religious Freedom Act (IRFA).[*]

Although there has been a substantial reduction in violence in Iraq since the Commission reported last in May 2007, there has been continued targeted violence, as well as threats and intimidation against persons belonging to religious minorities, and other egregious religiously-motivated abuses are continuing and widespread. The lack of effective government action to protect these communities from abuses has established Iraq among the most dangerous places on earth for religious minorities.

While there has been some reconciliation between Shi'a and Sunni Iraqis, there are still concerns regarding attacks and tense relations between these groups. Moreover, the situation is particularly dire for Iraq's smallest religious minorities, including ChaldoAssyrian Christians, other Christians, Sabean Mandaeans, and Yazidis. These groups do not have militia or tribal structures to protect them and do not receive adequate official protection. Their members continue to experience targeted violence and to flee to other areas within Iraq or other countries, where the aforementioned minorities represent a disproportionately high percentage among Iraqi refugees. These communities report that their numbers in Iraq have substantially diminished, and that their members who have left the country have not to date showed signs of returning in significant numbers. Legally, politically, and economically marginalized, these small minorities are caught in the middle of a struggle between the Kurdistan Regional Government (KRG) and the central Iraqi government for control of northern areas where their communities are concentrated. The combined effect of all of this has been to endanger these ancient communities' very existence in Iraq.

---

[*] Commissioners Cromartie, Eid, Land, and Leo do not rule out the possibility that a CPC determination might be warranted in the context of a country that is at war, but, for the following reasons, do not believe that the standards of IRFA are satisfied here. To be deemed a country of particular concern under IRFA, the Government of Iraq must have "engaged in" or "tolerated" violations of religious freedom that are not only "egregious," but "systematic" and "ongoing" as well. Government action, complicity, or willful indifference must be established. The terms "systematic" and "ongoing" require demonstrating a pattern or practice of recurring violence that is readily discernible.

In Iraq at present, the aggressor that seeks to extinguish religious minorities is not the government in Baghdad, but rather, terrorist and insurgent groups. Commissioners Cromartie, Eid, Land, and Leo agree with the other five Commissioners that the Government of Iraq has not done what it needs to do in order to address the alarming plight of Iraq's Christian and other religious minority communities or, for that matter, to deal with what appear to be abusive or indifferent practices by the Kurdistan Regional Government (KRG). But this stems from a serious lack of capacity, continued shifts in the war's key flashpoints, and the KRG's longstanding insulation from Baghdad and the rest of the country with the initiation of the Gulf War in 1990 and subsequent no-fly zone in 1991. In other words, the requisite intent and a discernible pattern of recurring affirmative acts of abuse are not present.

The Commission unanimously recommends that the U.S. government should take a number of specific steps described on pages 32 - 39 of this report, that are designed to ensure:

- safe and fair provincial elections,
- security and safety for all Iraqis,
- the prevention of abuses against religious minorities is a high priority,
- the KRG upholds minority rights,
- U.S. financial assistance is refocused,
- religious extremism is countered and respect for human rights is promoted, and
- the situation of internally displaced persons and refugees is effectively addressed.

Introduction

Following the fall of the Ba'athist regime led by Saddam Hussein and brief period of rule by the U.S.-led Coalition Provisional Authority, the United States returned sovereignty to the Iraqi people in June 2004 under the terms of UN Security Council Resolution 1546. That resolution endorsed the formation of an interim Iraqi government, which was then followed by parliamentary elections in January 2005. Boycotted by many Sunni groups, those elections brought a Shi'a majority government to power in coalition with Kurdish parties. United States and foreign military forces subsequently remained in Iraq at the Iraqi government's invitation to support the new regime and help fight international terrorism.[2]

The outcome of the 2005 parliamentary elections reinforced Kurdish autonomy from Iraq's central government while at the same time hardening sectarian divisions between Iraq's Sunni and Shi'a communities. These divisions quickly evolved into sustained armed clashes between Sunni and Shi'a factions and widespread, religiously-motivated attacks on Iraqi civilians, particularly after the significant February 2006 bombing of Samarra's Al-Askari Mosque. By March 2007, sectarian violence in Iraq had grown so severe that some analysts described the situation as a civil war.[3]

Iraqis from many religious communities, Muslim and non-Muslim alike, have suffered violent attacks in the sectarian strife that has engulfed Iraq, but those from Iraq's smallest religious minorities—particularly ChaldoAssyrian Christians, other Christians, Sabean Mandaeans, and Yazidis—have been among the most vulnerable. These groups were also targets of harassment and abuse during Saddam's era and their situation has grown more severe. The small religious communities do not have militia or tribal structures to provide them some level of protection. Indeed, their members appear to comprise a disproportionately large number of the multitude of refugees who have fled Iraq in the past several years.

As of mid-2007, when the Commission last reported on Iraq, the country was rife with growing levels of sectarian violence, including religiously-motivated killings, abductions, beatings, rape, intimidation, forced resettlement, torture, and attacks on pilgrims, religious leaders, and holy sites. Since 2007, actions and policies taken by the American and Iraqi governments and militaries have substantially diminished sectarian violence between the two major Islamic communities, Sunnis and Shi'as, and have led to progress in their political reconciliation. Serious concerns still remain, however, regarding abuses affecting each of these communities.

In contrast, the situation of the smallest religious minorities in Iraq has continued to deteriorate. Members of these small minorities continue to experience targeted attacks and to flee the country or to other areas within it. Aside from the Nineveh Plains and other areas in northern Iraq, much of the country, including Baghdad, has largely been emptied of Christians and other non-Muslims. Yet even in their northern ancestral homelands, these minorities remain subject to religiously-motivated extremist attacks and violence; compounding this are reports of an ongoing pattern of official discrimination and neglect at the hands of Iraqi and Kurdish authorities. The cumulative effect of this violence, forced displacement, discrimination, marginalization, and neglect is a serious threat to these ancient communities' continued existence in Iraq, where they have lived for millennia. This threat to Iraq's smallest religious minorities poses a grave threat to Iraq's future as a diverse and free society.

Commission Process

This report sets forth the conclusions and recommendations of the U.S. Commission on International Religious Freedom (USCIRF) with respect to violations of religious freedom conditions in Iraq, as well as U.S. policy toward the country. The report is based on Commission travel, interviews, briefings, and other activities undertaken in 2007 and 2008.

In July and September 2007, the Commission held public hearings on Capitol Hill focusing on the status of religious freedom in Iraq. The first hearing examined threats to Iraq's smallest religious minorities. Commissioners heard testimony from representatives of Iraq's Chaldean, Assyrian, and Sabean Mandaean communities, including a former Iraqi Minister of Human Rights. The hearing also featured an account from the Reverend Canon Andrew White, Vicar of Baghdad's only functioning ecumenical Christian parish, whose testimony included a description of the grave danger posed to the tiny remnant of Iraq's once sizable Jewish community. Statements were also made by Reps. Christopher Shays (R-CT) and Anna Eshoo (D-CA).

The second hearing focused on links between sectarian violence and the Iraqi refugee crisis. Commissioners heard testimony from security analysts, as well as from the office of the UN High Commission for Refugees, Assistant Commissioner for Operations Judy Cheng-Hopkins and Assistant Secretary of State for Population, Refugees, and Migration Ellen R. Sauerbrey. Commissioners also took statements from Senators Arlen Specter (R-PA) and Gordon Smith (R-OR), as well as Rep. Steve Israel (D-NY).

In November 2007, Commission staff traveled to Jordan and Sweden, and in March and May 2008, Commissioners traveled to Jordan, Iraq, and Syria to meet with Iraqi asylum seekers, refugees, and internally displaced persons (IDPs), including members of Iraq's smallest religious minorities, and various Iraqi and U.S. government officials. Seeking to gather information on religious freedom conditions and religiously-motivated violence in Iraq, the Commission learned from scores of officials, experts, and refugees about the circumstances under which displaced Iraqis fled their previous homes, as well as about the status and treatment of members of religious minorities in Iraq. The Commission also met with representatives of international and non-governmental organizations that are assisting asylum seekers, refugees, and IDPs. In Erbil, Iraq, the Commission met with members of the Kurdistan Regional Government (KRG) and local government officials, representatives of local religious communities, human rights organizations, and political parties. The Commission also met with U.S. Ambassador to Iraq Ryan Crocker and other U.S. officials, to discuss religious freedom issues in both Kurdish-dominated areas and other parts of Iraq. In April 2007, Commission staff met with Iraqi Christian asylum seekers in Detroit.

In preparing this report, the Commission also received briefings from Iraq experts; met with Secretary of State Condoleezza Rice, other U.S. government officials, representatives from international organizations, non-governmental organizations (NGOs), and universities; had several video conferences with key U.S. and Iraqi government officials and minority community leaders in Baghdad;[4] and reviewed reports on Iraq from the U.S. government, UN agencies, NGOs, the press, and other sources. Additionally, the Commission's previous findings and reports were consulted.

Religious Freedom Conditions

When the Commission last reported on Iraq in May 2007, the country was wracked with growing levels of sectarian violence, including religiously-motivated killings, abductions, beatings, rape, intimidation, forced resettlement, torture, and attacks on pilgrims, religious leaders, and holy sites.[5] Since that time, there has been a sizable drop in inter-communal violence between Sunni and Shi'a communities in Iraq, which can be attributed to some or all of the following factors: the "surge" in the number of U.S. troops and resulting increased security and counter-insurgency efforts; the improving abilities of the Iraqi Security Forces (ISF); the results of what is reported to be a secret U.S. program to identify and kill terrorist and insurgent leaders; the effects of the Sunni "Awakening"/Sons of Iraq movement and its political cooperation due to U.S. financial support; the ceasefire imposed by Shi'a cleric Muqtadeh al-Sadr on his Mahdi Army militia; and the *de facto* sectarian partition of neighborhoods, which in some cases resulted from forced displacement and in others from anticipatory, voluntary flight.[6]

According to the Pentagon's most recent quarterly report on security in Iraq, released in late September 2008, overall civilian deaths countrywide in June through August 2008 had declined 77 percent from the same period in 2007, with June recording the lowest monthly death rate on record since the war began.[7] Although ethno-sectarian killings increased slightly in July and August from the June statistics, they were reported to be 96 percent lower than in the same period in 2007. Total attacks and other security incidents were at their lowest levels since early 2004. Nevertheless, the report cautioned that despite reduced numbers, the situation remains "fragile, reversible, and uneven," and correctly noted that Iraq is still in the throes of "a communal struggle for power and resources." This report and others identify the major continuing threats to security in Iraq as including the actions of al-Qaeda in Iraq (AQI) and other extremist and insurgent elements, including Iranian-backed militias; the integration of the Sons of Iraq into the army, police or other jobs; the status of Kirkuk and other disputed areas;[8] the return of refugees and internally displaced persons (IDPs); and the lack of government services and economic opportunity. While violence could flare up at any time, U.S. Secretary of Defense Robert Gates and others warn that it is particularly probable in the run-up to provincial elections, scheduled for January 31, 2009.[9]

According to Iraqi government statistics, for the months since the Pentagon report, 359 Iraqi civilians were killed in September 2008, compared to 382 in August and 884 in September of last year.[10] In October 2008, 278 civilians were killed, which Iraqi officials said was the lowest monthly statistics since before the February 2006 Samarra bombings, and 296 were killed in November, when there was an uptick in bombings in Baghdad.[11]

Violence and Abuses Against Non-Muslim Minorities

Iraq's non-Muslim religious minorities—particularly Christians, Mandaeans, and Yazidis—have suffered religiously-based attacks and other abuses, and have fled the country, at rates far disproportionate to their numbers, seriously threatening these communities' continued existence in Iraq. Lacking militias, and in the case of the Mandaeans unable to defend themselves for religious reasons, they are easy prey for extremists and criminals, and they do not receive adequate protection from the authorities. As in earlier years, they also are caught in the middle of a Kurdish-Arab struggle for control of disputed northern areas where the minorities are concentrated and have been targeted because of this.

In addition to lacking security, these communities are legally, politically, and economically marginalized. In the January 2005 elections, many non-Muslims in Nineveh governorate—the northern province with the largest numbers of these groups—were disenfranchised due to fraud, intimidation, and the refusal by Kurdish security forces to permit ballot boxes to be distributed.[12] The Iraqi Constitution, adopted in late 2005, gives Islam a preferred status, providing a potential justification for abuses and discrimination against non-Muslims, and constitutional reform efforts have been stalled for several years. Most recently, the provincial elections law passed in late September 2008 by the Iraqi parliament was, at the last minute, stripped of Article 50, a provision that would have guaranteed a set number of seats in provincial councils to minorities. Although an amendment was later adopted, it set aside fewer seats than the original provision, leading minority leaders to denounce the law. Members of these groups also report that their communities are discriminated against in the provision of essential government services and reconstruction and development aid.

Christians

In 2003, there were estimated to be as many as 1.4 million Christians in Iraq, including Chaldean Catholics, Assyrian Orthodox, Assyrian Church of the East, Syriac Orthodox, Armenians (Catholic and Orthodox), Protestants, and Evangelicals. Today, it is thought that only 500,000 to 700,000 indigenous Christians remain in the country.[13] Moreover, while Christians and other religious minorities represented only approximately three percent of the pre-2003 Iraqi population, they constitute approximately 15 and 20 percent of registered Iraqi refugees in Jordan and Syria, respectively, and Christians account for 35 and 64 percent, respectively, of all registered Iraqi refugees in Lebanon and Turkey. Christian leaders have warned that the result of this flight may be "the end of Christianity in Iraq."[14]

The most recent attacks took place in the northern city of Mosul in late September/early October 2008, when at least 14 Christians were killed and many more report they were threatened, spurring some 13,000 individuals to flee to villages east and north of the city[15] and an estimated 400 families to flee to Syria.[16] The United Nations has estimated that this number is half of the current Christian population in Mosul. Those who met with displaced Christians were told that Christians had received threatening text messages and had been approached by strangers asking to see their national identity cards, which show religious affiliation. At the time of this writing, the attackers had not been identified, and Christian leaders had called for an international investigation. As of early November, some of the displaced reportedly were beginning to return to Mosul,[17] but a November 11 attack in which two Christian girls were killed, their mother injured, and their home bombed created new fears and slowed this trend. Reportedly, returnees and those who remained in Mosul fear future attacks against their community and maintain a low profile.[18]

The UN recently reported that from January through June 2008 it received 17 reports of attacks and kidnappings, including 10 killings, of Christians throughout Iraq.[19] In February, Christian missionaries from the Norwegian Churches Organization were kidnapped from Basra's Al Sakhra Church.[20] In July 2008, the Assyrian International News Agency (AINA) reported that a group called "The Battalion of Just Punishment, Jihad Base in Mesopotamia," which is thought to be affiliated with AQI, was sending threatening letters to Christians in the Mosul area.[21] On September 2, two Christians were kidnapped and killed in Mosul, apparently in separate incidents, including a doctor whose family paid a ransom of $20,000.[22]

According to Christian advocacy groups, since 2004, more than 40 churches and church buildings in Iraq have been destroyed, many in coordinated attacks, and others have been looted or occupied by Muslims.[23] The non-governmental organization, Minority Rights Group International, has reported that many of these attacks have been carried out during services to achieve maximum impact.[24] On August 1, 2004 four churches in Baghdad and one in Mosul were attacked simultaneously by the "Committee of Planning and Follow-up in Iraq" in retribution for what the group perceived to be "crusading" by the Christians and Americans.[25] In January 2006, churches in Baghdad, Mosul, and Kirkuk and the Vatican embassy were attacked on the same day, killing 16 and injuring 20 people. As recently as January 8, 2008, six church buildings in Mosul and Baghdad were bombed in a single day. These coordinated attacks fell on Epiphany and Orthodox Christmas Eve, feast dates when many Catholic and Syriac Orthodox Iraqis hold baptisms.[26] Some churches in Baghdad are now guarded by privately hired security firms,[27] and many have taken down their crosses.[28]

Christian leaders have been murdered, tortured, kidnapped, and beaten as a means to intimidate the entire community.[29] There have been reports that in some particularly dangerous areas, some priests stopped wearing their clerical garb for fear of attack.[30] On February 29, 2008, unidentified gunmen abducted the Chaldean Archbishop of Mosul, Paulos Faraj Rahho, and killed two of his aides. Archbishop Rahho's body was found in a shallow grave two weeks later. In early April 2008, an Assyrian Orthodox priest, Youssef Adel, was shot and killed in a drive-by attack in Baghdad.[31]

Christian laypersons also have been targeted, and congregations are reported to be less than half their pre-2003 levels, either because Christians have left the area or because those who remain are too afraid to attend church. Many churches have closed. In his testimony before the Commission in July 2007, Rev. Canon White, Vicar of St. George's Anglican Church in Baghdad, recounted that:

> Two weeks ago, I sat down with my congregation … and I said to them, tell me your story, what's happened in the past week? And the people went through what had happened, and I realized that 36 of my congregation in that past week had been kidnapped. None of them had been returned. The only one we managed to get back was one of our lay pastors, because we had found sufficient money to pay the ransom for his return.[32]

Although some observers have argued that Iraqi Christians are targeted for kidnapping because of their wealth, not their religious identity, relief groups have reported that, in many of these cases, a religious motivation is clear from the threats and ransom notes.[33] The Commission was told of and shown such threats and notes in its meetings with Iraqi Christian refugees in Jordan. Christians also have reported, including to the Commission, being targeted because, as Christians, they are considered "infidels" or are perceived to be affiliated with, or at least sympathetic to, the U.S. "Crusaders" who invaded Iraq.[34]

Extremists also have tried to enforce restrictive forms of Islamic behavior and dress on Christians. Christian women have been forced to wear the *hijab* and some forced to leave their positions of employment because of their failure to do so. Women have been threatened and even killed for socializing publicly with men who are not their relatives. Businesses that are considered "un-Islamic," including alcohol shops, beauty salons, cinemas, and video stores, and their Christian owners, have been intimidated and attacked. The State Department reports that as recently as February 26, 2008, a bomb exploded in front of a liquor store in Baghdeda, an Assyrian town.[35] Iraqi officials have reported that 95 percent of businesses that sold alcohol in Baghdad, Mosul and Basra (businesses commonly owned by Christians and Yazidis) have been closed.[36] Such reports were confirmed to the Commission on its trip to Jordan, where minority refugees told of being threatened because of their ownership of certain types of businesses. These individuals fled the country after receiving threatening letters and phone calls, and in some cases, after surviving violent attacks (including bombings) of their businesses.[37]

Threats and attacks have forced many Christians from their homes. A primary example of forced displacement can be found in Baghdad's previously mixed neighborhood of Dora, where reportedly only 300 Christian families remained in the summer of 2007, out of the 2,000 that had lived there previously.[38] One news report described the situation in Dora:

> ...a fatwa was issued and letters [were] distributed to Christians in the Dora neighborhood of Baghdad read[ing], "To the Christian, we would like to inform you of the decision of the legal court of the Secret Islamic Army to notify you that this is the last and final threat. If you do not leave your home, your blood will be spilled and your family will be killed." Christians in Dora also report posters being put up in the neighborhood stating that Christians are opposed to Islam, they are infidels, and warning women that unless they wear the *hijab* they would have their heads cut off.[39]

According to the UN Assistance Mission for Iraq (UNAMI), militants from extremist organizations, including the Islamic State of Iraq and the so-called "Mujahideen al-Dora," traveled door to door in the neighborhood, presenting Christians with the option of vacating their homes, paying the *jizyah* (a protection tax required to be paid by non-Muslims under some interpretations of Islamic law), or converting to Islam.[40] Similar threatening notes were shown to the Commission by refugees in Amman. In his July 2007 testimony before the Commission, Rev. Canon White stated that many Christians who fled their homes after receiving threats to convert, leave or die had nowhere else to go, and as a result, "a large number of Assyrians are now literally living on the church floors of some of the Assyrian churches in Baghdad."[41]

Donny George, the former Director General of the Iraqi Museums and Chairman of the State Board of Antiquities and Heritage, testified before the Commission that:

> After the Americans toppled Saddam's power in April 2003, everybody started breathing the freedom and waiting for democracy to start and everyone as an Iraqi should have his rights. But the infiltration of people coming from the countries surrounding Iraq made it impossible to start the real process of improving the situation in the country. Besides fighting each other, the Sunnis and Shi'as, a large campaign started against the Christians. At home, at my parents' place in Dora, we started hearing that the Muslim extremists will do to the Christians exactly what they did to the Jews in 1948. This meant complete cleansing of the people from the county. We received a letter in an envelope together with bullet of a Kalashnikov; the letter threatened my younger son, Martin, accusing him of cursing Islam and teasing Muslim girls. They mentioned that they suspected that his father, myself, works with the Americans, so he was ordered to write a letter of apologize (sic) for them, (the Brigades of the Martyr Zarqawi), and a fine of one thousand U.S. dollars, to be put in an envelope and dropped in a certain place in Dora, otherwise, the next day he will be kidnapped and beheaded immediately. When I heard that, I asked my elder son to get my mother, my two sisters and Martin and bring them to our flat in another part of Baghdad, and in the afternoon I arranged for the letter and the money to be dropped, so that they will not come after my son. In the coming few days, I heard that the same thing had happened to 12 Christian families in the same area of Dora, same kind of letter and the same kind of accusations. They all paid and left the area, leaving everything behind, houses, properties. Now Dora is completely empty of any Christian Assyrians, and almost all the churches there had been bombed and burnt.[42]

More recently, however, several official actions and related events have been taken to address these negative trends for Christians and the other small minorities. In 2007, some Christians openly celebrated Christmas Mass in Baghdad.[43] The State Department also reported that in 2007, a cross was reinstalled on one of the major churches in Dora,[44] and the Iraqi press has reported that 45 Christian families have returned to the neighborhood.

On several occasions in 2007 and 2008, including after the late September/early October attacks in Mosul, Iraqi Prime Minister Nuri al-Maliki met with Christian leaders to express support and pledged to protect Iraqi Christians.[45] In the wake of the Mosul violence, the Prime Minister also dispatched additional police officers to that area. In March 2008, when the Chaldean Archbishop of Mosul was kidnapped, Prime Minister al-Maliki stated that securing Archbishop Rahho's release was a "top priority" of the Iraqi government. After the Archbishop was found dead, the Prime Minister condemned the killing.[46] A suspect in the killing was arrested shortly thereafter, and by mid-May, the Iraqi Central Criminal Court had convicted the suspect and sentenced him to the death penalty.[47]

In June 2008, the Prime Minister established a committee to advise him on minority issues, reportedly including Christians and Yazidis, although the committee's specific membership, duties, and powers remain undisclosed. However, in recent meetings with representatives of Iraqi religious minority communities, the Commission was told that many in these communities view this committee as illegitimate because its members were selected by the Prime Minister, not by the communities themselves, and they feel that its members do not actively advance minority concerns. Additionally, the Mandaean representative with whom the Commission met was completely unaware of the Prime Minister's committee or if his community is represented on it.

Also in June 2008, Iraqi Vice President Tareq Al-Hashemi met with Mandaean spiritual leader Skeikh Ganzabra Sattar Jabbar Al-Hilo al-Zahrony.[48] On July 1, the Ministry of Human Rights issued a report listing the number of deaths in different minority communities caused by targeted or indiscriminate attacks between 2003 and the end of 2007, as well as the numbers of internally displaced persons for each minority.[49] This is the first official Iraqi government public report on the plight of minorities in post-Saddam Iraq.

Finally, in the wake of the September passage of the provincial elections law, majority politicians, including Prime Minister al-Maliki and Nassar al-Rubaiy'i, the leader of the Sadrist bloc, as well as some senior Muslim religious leaders, expressed concern about the deletion of Article 50, the minority representation provision. However, as mentioned previously, the replacement clause that was later adopted set aside fewer seats for minorities than the deleted provision, causing dissatisfaction among the minorities.

Mandaeans

Sabean Mandaeans, who are followers of John the Baptist, have seen their small community in Iraq decimated, with almost 90 percent reportedly having either fled the country or been killed.[50] Reportedly, only 3,500 to 5,000 Mandaeans (including 150 families in Baghdad) are now left in Iraq. Of the 28 Mandaean religious leaders who were in the country during the Saddam Hussein era, only five remain.[51] The community's highest spiritual leader fled to Syria following direct threats to his life.[52] The few Mandaeans who remain in the central and southern parts of the country are said to hide their religion. The Commission was told that some felt pressured to, and eventually did, change their religion.[53]

Like Christians, Mandaeans in Iraq have experienced threats, violence, forced expulsion from their homes and businesses, and violent attacks on their houses of worship and religious leaders. According to the Mandaean Human Rights Group, from April 2003 to March 2007, 144 Mandaeans were killed in Iraq, 254 were kidnapped, 238 were threatened or assaulted, 11 reported being raped, and there were 35 reports of forced conversion to Islam.[54] From January 2007 to February 2008 alone, the Mandaean community in Iraq suffered 42 killings, 46 kidnappings, 10 threats, and 21 attacks.[55] Speaking before the Commission in July 2007, Suhaib Nashi of the Mandaean Associations Union recounted a number of incidents in 2007 in which cars and buses were stopped by extremists and the Mandaeans were taken aside and killed on the side of the road while the Muslims were free to continue on their journey.[56]

Other human rights monitors also have reported abduction, rape, forced conversion, and forced marriage among young Mandaean women.[57] Like Christian women, Mandaean women have been forced to wear the *hijab*. Mandaeans report that their boys have been kidnapped and forcibly circumcised, a sin in the Mandaean religion.[58] Mandaean-owned jewelry shops and their owners have been attacked for being "un-Islamic." Mandaeans in Iraq also have experienced violent attacks on their places of worship and leaders. For example, on July 21, 2007, militants machine-gunned a Mandaean temple in Umara, injuring three religious leaders. Some Mandaeans reported to the Commission that they were too afraid to go to their temples.[59] Minority Rights Group International also has reported efforts to forcibly convert Mandaean leaders as a means to force them to encourage other community members also to convert.[60]

More recently, on September 26, the Mandaean Associations Union reported that earlier in the month, masked gunmen attacked a Mandaean family's shop in Baghdad, killing the owner, his brother, and his eight-year-old son, and looting the shop.[61] On February 2, 2008, 10 members of a Mandaean family in Kut were killed in a rocket attack. In Syria, the Commission met with family members of the deceased and was told that this family, the only Mandaean family in Kut, had received many threats and warnings from extremists before the attack.[62]

Mandaeans are pacifists whose religion prohibits them from carrying weapons or taking another person's life; as such, they have no means of self-defense and are therefore especially vulnerable. In addition, one can become Mandaean only by being born into the religion. Mandaean leaders have told the Commission that they are fearful that their ancient religion, language, and culture will disappear, not only in Iraq, but worldwide.[63] In 2006, the UN Education, Scientific, and Cultural Organization (UNESCO) listed Mandaean as one of the world's languages in danger of disappearing. The Mandaean Associations Union, Mandaean leaders, refugees, and asylum seekers have universally told the Commission that they do not see any future for their community in Iraq. All of the Mandaean refugees and asylum seekers with whom the Commission spoke said that they do not plan ever to return to Iraq. Instead, they would like the entire community to be resettled to a third country, so that their religion, language, and culture can survive.[64]

Yazidis

Almost the entire Yazidi population lives in northern Iraq, in the governorates of Dahuk and Nineveh. Like Mandaeans, Yazidis as a community are particularly vulnerable to annihilation because one can only be born into the Yazidi religion.[65]

Yazidis, Yazidi leaders, and Yazidi sites in Iraq have suffered threats and attacks since at least 2004.[66] Yazidis, whose religion is thought to be an derivative of Zoroastrianism, although it also includes elements of Judaism, Christianity, and other religions Islam,[67] are not viewed as "people of the Book;" extremists therefore consider them infidels or "sorcerers" and have called for their death. Minority Rights Group International reports that there were 25 reported killings of and 50 reported violent crimes targeting Yazidis from September to December 2004.[68] These incidents included two men being beheaded days after being threatened by conservative Muslims for failing to abide by a smoking ban during Ramadan.[69] In Mosul in March 2004, flyers could be found stating that divine awards awaited those who killed Yazidis[70] and in 2007, the Islamic State of Iraq, an extremist group with reported ties to al-Qaeda in Iraq, issued a fatwa calling for all Yazidis to be killed.[71] In September 2004, the Yazidi spiritual leader survived a bombing attack in Aif Sifni. The Commission was told by one Yazidi refugee that he was followed for several weeks by Islamic extremists on his way to and from work. After he started receiving threatening letters, he became so fearful for his life that he fled the country with his wife and children.[72] Yazidi cultural buildings and private property were damaged after dozens of Kurds attacked Shaikhan in retribution for two Yazidi men being found in a car with a married Kurdish woman in 2007.

On April 22, 2007, unidentified gunmen killed 23 Yazidis from the Kurdish town of Bashika. Reportedly, the gunmen stopped a bus outside of Mosul, discerned the Yazidis on the bus from their identity cards, told all other passengers to get off the bus, and drove the Yazidi men to eastern Mosul, where they were lined up against a wall and executed.[73] Yazidi refugees told the Commission that after this incident, members of their community in Mosul started receiving threatening letters, spurring many to flee the city.[74] The scale of the attacks against Yazidis increased dramatically on August 14, 2007, when four coordinated suicide bombings in the northern Yazidi towns of Qahtaniya and Jazeera killed 796 civilians and wounded another 1,562. The attack, which destroyed the two towns and left more than 1,000 Yazidi families homeless,[75] followed growing tensions between Yazidis and Sunnis, exemplified by letters and leaflets condemning Yazidis as "infidels" and "anti-Islamic."[76] The UN has recently reported that, in the first half of 2008, at least 5 Yazidis were killed in Sinjar.[77] On December 7, 2008, two Yazidis reportedly were killed in a liquor store in Mosul.[78] On the night of December 14, 2008, seven members of a Yazidi family were gunned down in their home in Sinjar.[79]

Minority Rights Group International reports that those Yazidis who remain in Iraq are fearful of traveling outside their communities, which has led many farmers to lose their livelihoods because they no longer go to markets to sell their produce.[80] Yazidis with whom the Commission met report members of the community having to depend on middlemen to sell their produce.[81] Many Yazidis have been attacked for owning alcohol shops, although *The New York Times* has reported that some Yazidis opened liquor businesses in Baghdad in late 2007.[82] Yazidis have reported to the Commission that Muslims refuse to frequent their businesses or businesses that employ Yazidis because Muslims consider them to be "dirty."[83] Many Yazidis have stopped performing religious ceremonies, fearful of being attacked.[84] Yazidis also complain of being underrepresented in local government and of their representatives being barred from or ignored in meetings.[85]

Other Minorities

Iraq's small Baha'i community, which is estimated to have 2,000 members, has experienced repression stemming from its prohibited legal status. Law No. 105 of 1970 continues to prohibit the practice of the Baha'i faith. However, in a positive move, in April 2007, the Iraqi Ministry of Interior cancelled Regulation 358 of 1975, which had prohibited the issuance of national identity cards to Baha'is, and the State Department has reported that a small number of Baha'is were issued identity cards in 2007.[86] Nevertheless, Iraqi identity cards continue to explicitly note the holder's religion and Baha'is, whose identity cards were changed to read "Muslim" after Regulation 358 was instituted, as well as Muslims who convert to Christianity, continue to be unable to change their cards to reflect their Baha'i or Christian faith.

Iraq's ancient and once large Jewish community now numbers fewer than 10, who reportedly live essentially in hiding. Many Jews left Iraq in the years following the founding of the state of Israel, and a law passed in March 2006 precludes Jews who emigrated from regaining Iraqi citizenship.[87] According to the State Department, anti-Semitism remains a "cultural undercurrent" in Iraq.[88] In September 2008, the Iraqi government announced that it would prosecute member of parliament Mithal al-Alusi for the "crime" of traveling to Israel, an "enemy country" under a Saddam-era law that has not been enforced against anyone other than al-Alusi.[89] The parliament also voted to prevent al-Alusi from attending future parliamentary sessions or from traveling outside Iraq, and stripped him of his parliamentary immunity and parliament-funded body guards. On November 24, al-Alusi was acquitted by an Iraqi court, which ruled that his visit was not contrary to Iraqi law because passports no longer prohibited Iraqis from entering Israel.[90]

Minorities in Disputed Areas

The vast majority of non-Muslim minorities who have been displaced from other areas in Iraq have gone to the north, mainly to Nineveh governorate, where religious minorities represent 53 percent of the population,[91] and to the three governorates controlled by the Kurdistan Regional Government (KRG), Dahuk, Erbil and Sulaymaniyah. According to the International Organization for Migration (IOM), in Nineveh and the KRG, Christians represent 52.2 percent and 24.6 percent, respectively, of all IDPs who have fled to those areas.[92] Northern Iraq, particularly the Nineveh Plains area of Nineveh governorate, is the historic homeland of Iraq's Christian community, and the Yazidi community is indigenous to Nineveh and Dahuk. Moreover, the KRG region, as compared to the rest of Iraq, is relatively secure.

In the KRG itself, members of religious minority communities generally are not subject to violent persecution, and many Iraqi Christians and Mandaeans fleeing violence in other parts of Iraq have found safety there.[93] It has been easier for displaced Christians from other areas to settle in the three KRG governorates than for IDPs who are members of other communities. According to the KRG Minister of Interior, Christians undergo less stringent security checks because Christians are not seen as terrorists, but rather as victims fleeing terrorists.[94] However, as of December 1, 2008, the KRG eased its border restrictions on the entry of Iraqis from other areas of the country, although IDPs will still be required to have a local sponsor.

Christians, Mandaeans, and Yazidis in the KRG region also report that they are free to practice their religion, to establish private schools in their own language for their children, and to opt out of Islamic classes in public schools. Mandaean IDPs who have settled in Erbil told the Commission that they feel secure enough to have opened a Mandaean cultural center and have requested permanent residence in the KRG.[95] Additionally, during its mission to Erbil, the Commission was told by several Yazidis that Yazidis who live in the KRG proper feel more secure than those who live outside of the three KRG governorates.[96]

Nineveh governorate, however, especially in and around Mosul, remains one of the most dangerous and unstable parts of Iraq. Insurgent and extremist activity continues to be a significant problem there, and control of the ethnically and religiously mixed area is disputed between the KRG and the central Iraqi government. While violence overall in Iraq decreased in

2007 and 2008, the Mosul area remains what U.S. and Iraqi officials call the insurgents' and extremists' last urban stronghold, with continuing high levels of violence.[97] Increased security operations by U.S. and Iraqi forces have led to some decrease in the violence in and around Mosul, but the area remains very dangerous, as evidenced by the October attacks on Christian residents, which killed at least 14 Christians and spurred the flight of 13,000 from Mosul to surrounding areas. According to the September 2008 U.S. Department of Defense report to Congress, "[d]uring the past few years, Mosul has been a strategic stronghold for [al-Qaeda in Iraq (AQI)], which also needs Mosul for its facilitation of foreign fighters. The current sustained security posture, however, continues to keep AQI off balance and unable to effectively receive support from internal or external sources, though AQI remains lethal and dangerous."[98] According to the Special Inspector General for Iraqi Reconstruction, from April 1 to July 1, 2008, there were 1,041 reported attacks in Nineveh governorate and from July 1 to September 30, 2008, there were 924 attacks, still a significant number.[99]

This situation has been exacerbated by Arab-Kurdish tensions over control of Mosul and other disputed areas in Nineveh governorate. The dispute stems from Kurdish claims and efforts to annex territories—including parts of the governorates of Kirkuk (Tamim), Nineveh, Salah al-Din, Diyala, and Waset—into the KRG, on the basis of the belief that these areas historically belong to Kurdistan. During the Saddam Hussein era, Kurds and other non-Arabs were expelled from these areas under his policy of "Arabization." Since 2003, Kurdish *peshmerga* and political parties have moved into these territories, effectively establishing *de facto* control over many of the contested areas.[100] Key to integrating the contested areas into Kurdistan is Article 140 of the Iraqi Constitution, which calls for a census and referendum in the territories to determine their control.[101] In this context, military or financial efforts undertaken by either Kurdish officials or Arab officials (whether in Baghdad or local) is seen by the other group as an effort to expand control over the disputed areas, leading to political disputes and deadlock.

Religious and ethnic minorities in the disputed territories find themselves caught in this tug-of-war between the KRG and the central Iraqi government. According to the most recent report of the UN Secretary-General to the UN Security Council, "[a]s elections and decisions on disputed territories draw closer, various groups are maneuvering to influence and manipulate the population composition in their respective areas of interest. There is increasing concern regarding alleged attempts to exert undue influence on the demographics in Diyala, Tamim, and [Nineveh] governorates in particular. The [UNAMI] Human Rights Office has received numerous reports of families being forced to sell their property at low prices, and of the confiscation of their agricultural land and economic assets. Moreover an increasing number of threats against their leaders have been registered, prompting further concern regarding the rights and security of minority groups in the country."[102] Furthermore, the Secretary-General's report, as well as the most recent UNAMI Human Rights Report, state that the UN has received reports that members of minority groups have been forced to identify themselves as either Arabs or Kurds.[103]

The dispute over minority quotas in the provincial elections law is another example of minorities being caught in the middle of the Kurdish-Arab struggle. As previously discussed, in late September the Iraqi parliament stripped a provision, Article 50, guaranteeing a set number of minority seats in certain provincial councils, from the provincial elections law just before the law's passage. This led to protests from the minorities and calls from majority political leaders, including Prime Minister al-Maliki, for the provision's reinstatement. A compromise amendment proposed by the UN would have set aside 12 minority seats in the Nineveh, Baghdad, and Basra provincial councils, but the amendment that was ultimately adopted by the parliament in early November provided for only six minority seats in these councils.[104] Reportedly, the reduction was because of Arab politicians' concerns that minorities would vote with the Kurds, thereby allowing the Kurds to expand their authority in the north.[105]

In its efforts to expand Kurdish control in the areas outside of the KRG region, KRG officials have come under scrutiny for abuses and discrimination against religious and ethnic minorities, including non-Muslims and ethnic Shabak and Turkomen. Kurdish officials reportedly have sent their *peshmerga* security forces into disputed areas, particularly in Nineveh and Kirkuk governorates, encroached on, seized, and refused to return minority land, made the provision of services and assistance to minority communities contingent on support for Kurdish expansion, and impeded the formation of local minority police forces.

To compensate for what they view as inadequate protection by Iraqi and Kurdish security forces, for several years Christians and Yazidis in northern Iraq have sought to establish representative community forces to police their own villages. However, according to news reports and as various interlocutors told the Commission, since 2006, a senior Kurdish official in Mosul— Khisro Goran, the Kurdistan Democratic Party (KDP) Deputy Governor of Nineveh Province— has blocked an order from the central government in Baghdad to train and deploy 700 Christian police recruits to guard their historic villages in the Nineveh Plains. Instead, the Christians who were recruited were sent to Mosul to fight AQI.[106] The Chaldean Assyrian Syriac Council of America (CASCA) has reported that Christians in the Nineveh Plains area who are interested in volunteering for the police have been discouraged by local Nineveh governorate authorities.[107] Additionally, the Commission has been told by representatives of the Christian community in Iraq that Christians who have been recruited into the police are not given the same opportunities for promotion as other officers and that they are marginalized within the force by being assigned to guard churches. Reportedly, some Christian churches in northern Iraq have begun organizing local "protection committees" to provide security in Christian areas. These forces are said to be funded by the KRG Minister of Finance, Sarkis Aghajan Mamendu, who is a Christian.

As of mid-2008, some progress appeared to have been made on bringing minorities into the Iraqi police force for the Nineveh Plains. Approximately 700 minority recruits had been vetted, and of these, 269 had been hired. This is consistent with the police recruit acceptance rate Iraq-wide, which is roughly one in three. The Commission has been told that Prime Minister al-Maliki is encouraging Christians to join the police force and in a meeting with church leaders asked them to provide a list of names of individuals interested in recruitment. However, some ChaldoAssyrian advocates continue to allege that the reason so few of the minority recruits have been hired is KRG interference and opposition, and that the hired recruits are not being provided with sufficient weapons, protective gear, vehicles, and uniforms.

The KRG Interior Minister also told the Commission in March 2008 that the KRG is working with the Yazidis to establish, recruit, and train a representative local police force for Yazidi areas.[108]

As in prior years, the State Department reported in 2008 that members of religious minority communities "living in areas north of Mosul, such as Yazidis and Christians, asserted that the KRG encroached on their property and illegally built Kurdish settlements on the confiscated land."[109] There also was a report that a prominent Patriotic Union of Kurdistan (PUK) official had said that Assyrians and Turkomen had no legitimate land claims in Kurdish-dominated territory.[110] In testimony before the Commission in July 2007, Michael Youash of the Iraq Sustainable Democracy Project said:

> Land theft, illegal land seizures, and the KRG's unwillingness to provide sufficient redress is perhaps one of the most single pressing issues at this time. Indeed, in some cases, very well placed networks within the KDP are behind the seizure of Christian lands.... Land seizures ... represent the dislocation of our people from their lands, the denial of their right to earn a livelihood, and the theft of a chance at realizing their potential. This is a direct effort at soft ethnic cleansing. [111]

While in Erbil, the Commission met with Christians and Yazidis who repeated land confiscation charges and asserted that the KRG was not implementing judicial decisions requiring the return of minority properties. Yousif Mohammed Aziz, the KRG Minister of Human Rights, confirmed to the Commission that he has received complaints of confiscated properties and said he had forwarded them to the KRG Ministry of Justice.[112] KRG Finance Minister Sarkis acknowledged these complaints and said that the Kurdish government has instituted a policy to compensate Kurds who return occupied houses and lands to Christians. The Finance Minister said he hopes that all properties would be returned to Christians within the next two years. Additionally, the Finance Minister explained that in the Ainkawa neighborhood of Erbil, only Christians can buy and sell land.[113]

In the effort to increase control over disputed areas, KRG officials reportedly have implemented various patronage systems in which aid is distributed only to those who pledge political loyalty. Some Christian churches and aid organizations have complained they are denied funding by the Kurdish government for assistance programs to IDPs because they have not pledged support to the KDP. A Christian advocacy organization reported that the KDP has been pressuring Christians to sign forms pledging their support for the Nineveh Plains area to be annexed to Kurdish areas and placed under KRG rule. The KDP is reported to be the only investor in the Yazidi community and provides significant investments in the cultural and religious activities in Yazidis, including support for the Yazidi Lalish Cultural Center and its employees; however, some argue that the KDP's support has led to a dependency and patronage system, at the expense of independent Yazidi political parties.[114] In addition, according to Minority Rights Group International, Yazidis have claimed that the Kurds have tried to "Kurdify" them in an effort to extend their control over Yazidi areas.[115] Finally, some minority groups report that they have been forced to identify themselves as either Kurdish or Arab to access some services.[116]

Political conflicts between Kurds and Arabs have also led to a stalemate in the distribution of Nineveh's provincial budget, with only 0.4 percent of the budget being spent in 2008, the lowest rate for any Iraqi governorate.[117] In October 2008, the Special Inspector General for Iraqi Reconstruction reported that "[U.S. Provincial Reconstruction Team] Ninewa reports that residents, especially those in rural areas, lack adequate access to essential services. Moreover, budget execution remains slow, and expenditure data is not being reported transparently."[118] And the Commission has been told that $100 million provided by Prime Minster al-Maliki for reconstruction in Mosul was not well spent and therefore did not have a discernible effect on efforts to reconstruct the city.

This political stalemate and failure to spend reconstruction and development assistance, as well as alleged political motives behind finance assistance provided by the KRG, have led minority communities in these areas to complain that they have been denied their fair share of social welfare and reconstruction aid. According to community representatives, they lack sufficient water, electricity, sanitation, health services, schooling, roads and other essential services.[119] Some groups claim that Kurdish officials have cut off water and power supplies to certain Christian villages, including the village of Humziya.[120] Yazidis claim that their villages are the last (after Muslim and Kurdish villages) to receive assistance to build schools or infrastructure.[121]

To address their lack of security and political and economic marginalization, some Iraqi minority groups, both inside and outside Iraq, have been campaigning for what is variously described as a protected, semi-autonomous, or autonomous area for Christians, and some say for other minorities as well, in the Nineveh Plains area. These options are being considered to give effect to Article 125 of the Iraqi Constitution, which "guarantee[s] the administrative, political, cultural and educational rights of the various nationalities, such as Turkomen, Chaldeans, Assyrians, and all other constituents," and provides that this "shall be regulated by" a future law. However, the specifics of what such a law would entail, including the territory that such an area would cover, its religious and ethnic make-up, how it would be secured, what governance and economic powers it would have, and how it would relate to the KRG and the central Iraqi government remain disputed even among those who say that they favor autonomy. The idea of greater autonomy for minorities in Iraq was recently discussed and endorsed, though with disagreement as to the details, by most members of Iraqi minority diaspora communities at a conference at George Washington University in November 2008. By contrast, some Iraqi minority individuals and groups with whom the Commission met in Iraq, Jordan, Syria, and Sweden, as well as a minority at the George Washington diaspora conference, oppose the idea.

The U.S. government has undertaken some efforts to address the concerns of Iraq's smallest minority communities, including distributing USAID funds of $11 million in fiscal year 2008 and slating $10 million for fiscal year 2009 to these communities, appointing a Special Coordinator on Minority Communities in Iraq at the State Department, and, in the spring of 2008, creating a U.S. government Inter-Agency Task Force on Iraqi minority issues. The Task Force was supposed to recommend specific policies to improve the situation of minorities in Iraq and, in the spring and summer of 2008, reportedly was working on a policy document. However, the Commission learned recently that there was no final agreement on the document and, as a result, no specific policies have been implemented. The Commission urges the U.S. government urgently to revive the interagency discussion of policy options for Iraqi minority communities and to adopt and implement specific policies to address the needs of these vulnerable communities.

Intra-Muslim Sectarian Violence and Abuses

<u>Shi'a Violence Against Sunnis</u>

Over the past several years, many serious sectarian abuses have been attributed to actors from the Shi'a-dominated Iraqi Ministry of Interior (MOI) and Ministry of Defense (MOD), and/or by armed Shi'a groups with ties to the Iraqi government or to elements within it. These groups have included al-Sadr's Mahdi Army,[122] as well as the Badr Brigade (now called the Badr Organization), which is affiliated with the Islamic Supreme Council in Iraq (ISCI). The ISCI is the political party that holds the largest bloc of seats in the Iraqi Council of Representatives and is the dominant faction in the United Iraq Alliance coalition that includes Prime Minister al-Maliki's Dawa party.[123] The apparent collusion between state security forces and para-state militias featured prominently in the Commission's 2007 *Annual Report*, as well as in the State Department's 2007 human rights and religious freedom reports. In its 2008 religious freedom report, covering the period from July 1, 2007 to June 30, 2008, the State Department reported that the "sectarian misappropriation of official authority within the [Iraqi government's] security apparatus . . . which had been a significant concern in earlier reporting periods, declined markedly this year." [124]

Nevertheless, reports in 2007 and 2008 make clear that continued improvements in this area are still needed. In September 2007, an independent, congressionally-mandated commission led by retired Marine General James L. Jones found that the Iraqi MOI was "dysfunctional and sectarian" and that the National Police were "highly sectarian" and should be disbanded.[125] In May 2008, a U.S. Institute of Peace report concluded that, although improvements had been made by the post-2006 Interior Minister and his Coalition advisors, "the U.S. remains far from its goal of creating an effective Interior Ministry and Iraqi police force that can protect all Iraqi citizens," and urged heightened efforts to improve the MOI's institutional capacity, to focus less on meeting the numbers of police recruited and more on quality and results, and to address the force's continuing sectarian imbalance.[126] In May, the U.S. Embassy in Baghdad reported continuing problems with the professionalism of the Iraqi police.[127] In June, a report by the Government Accountability Office concluded that sectarian and militia influences remained a problem undermining Iraq's security forces.[128] During the period January to April 2008, 14 Sunni men were kidnapped at police checkpoints in Al-Muqdadiyah, north of Baghdad, by criminal elements believed to include Iraqi police officers.[129]

On October 1, 2008, the Iraqi government began supervising the "Sons of Iraq" groups, starting with those in Baghdad province, which make up slightly more than half of these groups countrywide. Analysts, and many Iraqi Sunnis, view the government's future handling of these groups as a major test of its commitment to sectarian reconciliation.[130] In this regard, as noted in September by the U.S. Department of Defense, recent allegations of ISF targeting of Sons of Iraq in Diyala province are troubling.[131]

In October 2007, the United Nations Assistance Mission for Iraq (UNAMI) observed that Iraqi government "arrest sweeps conducted under the Baghdad Security Plan are often less targeted than is typically portrayed by the authorities," thereby wrongly detaining ordinary Sunni civilians. Further, UNAMI reported that detainees in some MOI prisons had been hung by their limbs, electrocuted, burned, forced to sit on sharp objects, and beaten with hoses, pipes, and other blunt instruments.[132] UNAMI also reported alleged abuses of female Sunni detainees, including beatings, rapes, and other forms of sexual assault by MOI personnel.[133] In March 2008, UNAMI recognized that the Iraqi government had taken steps to improve the handling of detainees, but it continued to express concern at, among other issues, the government's continuing "failure to promptly and thoroughly investigate credible allegations of torture and to institute criminal proceedings against officials responsible for abusing detainees."[134]

Similarly, the State Department's 2007 human rights report recounted numerous sectarian killings, torture, kidnappings, and other abuses by government agents, yet reported that, while there were some internal investigations, disciplinary actions, and/or re-trainings, "during the year no members of the security forces were tried or convicted in court in connection with alleged violations of human rights."[135] The Department's 2008 religious freedom report noted that "limitations in security force capabilities and in the country's rule of law infrastructure made it difficult for the [ISF] or the justice system to investigate and prosecute criminal activity, including alleged sectarian crimes."[136]

In recent months, Prime Minister al-Maliki said that he is committed to fighting so-called "special groups" and other armed Shi'a factions. On April 7, 2008, the Prime Minister denied supporting Shi'a militias, arguing that his government would not and "did not provide any sanctuary or opportunity for any outlaws, whether they were followers of the Mahdi Army or Muqtada al-Sadr or the Islamic Council or even of the Dawa party."[137] However, just three days before this declaration, Prime Minister al-Maliki issued a nationwide order freezing ISF raids against suspected militia groups.[138] In March 2008, the al-Maliki government launched a surprise offensive against Mahdi Army strongholds in Basra, touching off fighting between the government and the militia not only in the southern port city, but also in Baghdad's Sadr City and in Amara. The fighting continued until truces were agreed to in May and June.[139] The government also dismissed more than 1,300 soldiers who refused to fight the militia.[140] Some observers, however, have questioned whether Prime Minister al-Maliki undertook this offensive out of a real commitment to curb Shi'a militias or a desire to undermine a potential political rival before the upcoming elections.[141]

While the start of proceedings against two Health Ministry officials accused of supporting the Mahdi Army was initially claimed as evidence of the government's willingness to crack down on violations within its own ranks, their subsequent release after charges were dropped undermined this claim. Former Deputy Health Minister Hakim al-Zamili and Brig. Gen. Hameed al-Shimmari were arrested by U.S. forces in 2007, after allegedly using their positions to help Mahdi Army militiamen locate and execute Sunnis seeking treatment in public hospitals. Other charges included facilitating the torture and kidnapping of Sunni patients, arranging the use of public ambulances to transfer weapons, and participating in campaigns targeting Sunni doctors for extrajudicial killing.[142] Prosecutors also charged al-Zamili with diverting millions of dollars from the ministry to the Mahdi Army. However, government prosecutors dropped the charges in March 2008, citing a purported lack of evidence.[143]

<u>Sunni Violence Against Shi'a</u>

Serious sectarian abuses are still being committed by other organized groups outside of the government, notably the Sunni-dominated insurgency and indigenous and foreign extremist groups. Despite the decline in violence in the country, religiously-motivated insurgent and extremist attacks continued to occur in 2008. For example, on January 17, 2008, a suicide bomber killed eight religious pilgrims celebrating Ashura near a Shi'a mosque in Baquba, the capital of the volatile Diyala province. On February 15, two suicide bombers attacked a Shi'a mosque in the Turkomen town of Tal Afar in northern Iraq.[144] On February 24 and 25, suicide bombers targeted Shi'a pilgrims en route to Karbala for the festival of Arbaeen, killing 63 people and injuring more than 100. At the end of July, Shi'a pilgrims taking part in a festival in the Karrada section of Baghdad were targeted in a shooting that killed seven and, the following day, in coordinated suicide bombings that killed 32 and injured at least 64. And although Baghdad experienced the quietest Ramadan in three years, there still were five suicide attacks in the city during the late September/early October 2008 Eid al-Fitr holiday marking the end of the holy month, several of which were directed at Shi'a mosques.

Violence and Abuses Against Other Vulnerable Groups

Women and girls in Iraq also have suffered religiously-motivated abuses, including killings, abductions, rape, forced conversions, restrictions on movement, and forced marriages. Women who some considered to have violated Islamic teachings and other females who are politically active have been targeted by Sunni and Shi'a extremists alike.[145] Reportedly, some women have decided against running as candidates in the 2009 provincial elections fearing that they would be attacked.[146] Some parents reportedly have taken their daughters out of school, either fearing attacks or because they have been told that girls' education is forbidden by their religion. In October 2007, the Ministry of Education announced that the ratio of boys to girls in schools is now four to one.[147]

The UN Special Representative for Iraq, Staffan De Mistura, reported that more than 100 women were killed in southern Iraq in 2007.[148] Officials in Basra reported that 79 women were brutally murdered and in some cases tortured for alleged violations of Islamic teachings in that year. Such violations included refusing to wear the *hijab*, wearing makeup, and wearing western clothing.[149] There also have been reports of women being forced to divorce their husbands and remarry men in their own sect.[150]

Honor killings continue to be a serious problem in the Kurdish regions, where during the Commission's visit, the KRG Minister for Human Rights stated that the incidence of such crimes has continued to increase since 2005.[151] Figures published by the Ministry noted 118 murders of women in the first quarter of 2007 and 137 in the second,[152] and UN Special Representative De Mistura said that "at least" 300 women and girls were victims of honor crimes in the north in 2007, being shot, strangled or beaten to death.[153] Of those killed, 195 deaths were the result of burning—a tactic commonly associated with premeditated intra-family violence.[154] The UN reports that from January to June 2008, 56 women were murdered and 150 burned in Kurdistan, and that many of these instances followed the pattern of honor killings.[155] On the International Day on the Elimination of Violence against Women, the UN Special Rapporteur on Violence

Against Women reported that honor killings are among the primary causes of unnatural deaths among women in Northern Iraq and that incidents of self-immolation are increasing. Throughout the country, the Special Rapporteur said, perpetrators of honor killings, even if known, are rarely brought to justice.[156]

The KRG is attempting to address this problem. In July 2007, it created a commission to try to reduce honor killings and made changes to its laws to help ensure that perpetrators would be prosecuted and punished. The commission has subsequently established a board to monitor the implementation of the new laws.[157] However, the UN reports that prosecution is often hampered by insufficient evidence, reluctance of witnesses to testify, and courts granting leniency in the punishment of such crimes.[158]

Additionally, UNAMI has reported that the Women's Committee of the Kurdistan National Assembly (KNA) has drafted legislation to address a wide-ranging list of concerns to women, including underage and forced marriages, honor crimes, physical and other forms of violence, matrimonial entitlements, grounds for divorce, inheritance, and social status edicts found in the Personal Status Law.[159] In November 2008, the KNA passed amendments to the 1959 personal status law forbidding forced marriages and punishing relatives who forced unwanted or prevented wanted marriages.[160] Legislation to outlaw female circumcision with the imposition of jail terms and fines for offenders was introduced in the KNA,[161] and the week of November 19 was designated "Yes to gender equality, no to violence" week in the KRG.[162]

Honor killings were also reported among Iraq's minority religious communities. On April 7, 2007, a group of Yazidi men in Nineveh bludgeoned to death a 17-year-old Yazidi woman following allegations that she was engaged in a romantic relationship with a Muslim man. The incident touched off a wave of violence between Kurdish Muslims and northern Iraq's small Yazidi community, ultimately resulting in the extra-judicial killing of 23 Yazidi textile workers by unidentified gunmen on April 23.

Discrimination against women based on religious motivations also exists within the Iraqi government itself, where some officials reportedly have forced women to wear the *hijab* as a condition of employment, regardless of their religious affiliation.[163] In Amman, the Commission met with an Iraqi Christian refugee who testified that she was fired from her teaching position after refusing several times to wear the veil during her employment.[164] According to the State Department, education officials in Basra have instituted a policy requiring all females in the schools to cover their heads, and "all female university students in Mosul, even non-Muslims, were required to wear the *hijab*, or headscarf." The UN reports that some women have felt pressure to conform to more conservative forms of dress and behavior on certain militia-affiliated campuses to avoid harassment by guards.[165] Human rights monitors also have reported an increase in *de jure* and *de facto* government discrimination against women in the areas of divorce, inheritance, and marriage.[166]

Religiously-motivated violence also continues to be a serious threat to Muslims who reject orthodox interpretations of Islam, particularly legal and religious scholars targeted for their allegedly secular views and teachings. Academics have experienced persistent threats of kidnapping and murder (often along sectarian lines) and university campuses have been targets

21

of violent attacks.[167] According to the Iraqi Ministry of Higher Education, from 2003 to March 2007, more than 200 incidents of targeted assassinations and abductions of academic professionals were reported,[168] and the UN Scientific, Education, and Culture Organization (UNESCO) reported in 2007 that thousands of teachers had fled the country. There also are reports that Iraqi public universities and their departments have fractured along sectarian lines.[169]

Finally, as USCIRF has previously reported, homosexuals in Iraq have also been victims of religiously-motivated violence. In October 2005, Grand Ayatollah Ali Sistani issued a fatwa forbidding homosexuality and calling for gays and lesbians to be killed "in the most severe way." Subsequent reporting revealed the establishment of *ad hoc* religious tribunals led by Shi'a clerics, with penalties ranging from lashes to arbitrary killings.[170] Those reports were later verified by UNAMI.[171] In a May 2006 letter to a U.S.-based advocacy group, the U.S. State Department said that it was "troubled" by reports of "threats, violence, executions, and other violations of humanitarian law against members of the gay and lesbian community in Iraq."[172] Government actors are also suspected of this kind of targeted human rights violation. In 2007, members of Iraq's gay and lesbian community reported muggings, severe beatings and even rape by members of the Shi'a-dominated Iraqi Security Forces.[173]

The Plight of Iraqi Refugees and Internally Displaced Persons

The Extent and Causes of the Crisis

The confluence of sectarian violence, religious persecution, and other serious human rights violations has driven, by most estimates, more than 4.5 million Iraqis, or 20 percent of the Iraqi population,[174] from their homes to other areas of the country and countries outside Iraq.

According to the UN High Commissioner for Refugees (UNHCR), an estimated 2 million Iraqis have taken refuge in neighboring countries. Most left in the aftermath of the February 2006 bombing of the Al-Askari mosque in Samarra and the wave of sectarian violence that it unleashed. Of these, the vast majority are in Syria and Jordan.[175] As the influx of refugees increased in 2006 and 2007, straining public service resources, Syria, Jordan, Egypt, and Lebanon all imposed strict entry requirements. It is now almost impossible for Iraqi refugees to flee to these countries.

Members of Iraq's smallest religious minority communities, particularly ChaldoAssyrian Christians, Sabean Mandaeans, and Yazidis, appear to comprise a disproportionately high number of these refugees. Although they accounted for only approximately 3 percent of Iraq's pre-war total population, these minorities represent approximately 15 percent of the refugees who have registered to date with UNHCR in Jordan and 20 percent of refugees in Syria.[176] In Turkey and Lebanon, Christians represent 64 and 35 percent of registered refugees, respectively. Yazidis have fled overwhelmingly to Syria, where they represent approximately 0.7 percent of the registered refugees.[177] According to the Iraqi Ministry of Displacement and Migration (MoDM), almost half of Iraq's smallest religious minority population has fled abroad.

Large numbers of Muslims have fled abroad, as well. In Jordan, Sunni Muslims comprise 59 percent of the registered refugees while Shi'a Muslims make up only 27 percent. In Syria, Sunni Muslims represent 58 percent of the registered refugees and Shi'a Muslims 19.5 percent.[178]

There are also an estimated 2.8 million internally displaced persons (IDPs) within Iraq, more than half of whom were forcibly displaced or fled following the Samarra mosque bombing.[179] Iraqis displaced by sectarian violence within Iraq have moved primarily from religiously and ethnically mixed communities to homogeneous ones. Almost 65 percent of the IDPs have fled from homes in Baghdad, many moving to other neighborhoods in the capital and some going farther afield. The International Organization for Migration (IOM) reports that Shi'a Arabs represent 60 percent of IDPs, Sunni Arabs 28 percent, and ChaldoAssyrian Christians 5 percent of the IDP population.[180] Many Shi'a Muslims have moved from the center to the south of the country, and many Sunnis from the south to the upper-center of the country. The vast majority of Christians and members of other small religious minority communities have moved to the north, particularly the Nineveh governorate and the three KRG governorates, Dahuk, Erbil and Sulaymaniyah.[181]

IOM reported in November 2008 that in some isolated locations, new displacement continues, primarily due to military offensives, although not at the same rates as in 2006 and early 2007.[182] The reduced displacement has been attributed to improved security in some areas and the homogenization of formerly religiously mixed neighborhoods. In addition, many Iraqi governorates have imposed restrictions on outsiders' ability to relocate to their territories.

Between November 2007 and May 2008, the Commission traveled to Jordan, Iraq, Syria, and Sweden to meet with Iraqi asylum-seekers, refugees, and IDPs. These vulnerable and traumatized individuals provided accounts of kidnapping, rape, murder, torture, and threats to themselves, their families, or their community. While the vast majority of interviewees could not identify the perpetrators, they suspected various militias and extremist groups of committing these acts, and often provided specific identifying details.

Non-Muslim minority refugees told the Commission that they were targeted because they do not conform to orthodox Muslim religious practices and/or because, as non-Muslims, they are perceived to be working for the U.S.-led coalition forces. Members of these communities recounted how they, as well as other members of their families and communities, had suffered violent attacks, including murder, torture, rape, abductions for ransom or forced conversion, and the destruction or seizure of property, particularly businesses such as liquor stores or hair salons deemed un-Islamic. They also reported being forced to pay a protection tax and having been forced to flee their homes in fear after receiving threats to "convert, leave, or die." In addition, they told of their places of worship being bombed and forced to close and their religious leaders being kidnapped and/or killed.[183]

Sunni and Shi'a Muslim refugees told of receiving death threats, of family members being killed, of kidnappings, of their houses being burned down, and of forced displacements. Some refugees reported being targeted because of jobs held by them or their relatives, either connected to the U.S. government or to the Ba'athist regime. Other refugees spoke of being targeted because they were part of a mixed Muslim marriage or because their family was Sunni in a predominately

Shi'a neighborhood or vice versa. Many stated that the sectarian identities of their relatives and friends were either not known or not important before 2003, and several spoke of their families including both Sunnis and Shi'as and of the diverse nature of neighborhoods before the sectarian violence.[184] One refugee woman told the Commission that, after her son was kidnapped and returned to her, she received a phone call from a government official who knew the exact details of the kidnapping and who told her that her entire family should leave Iraq. When they got their visas to go to Syria, their passports were stamped "no return." Because of this incident, she alleged to the Commission that the government must have been involved in the violence directed at her family.[185]

A fall 2007 survey of 754 Iraqi refugees in Syria highlights the high degree of trauma that this population has suffered. Seventy-eight percent had a family member who had been killed between 2003 and the time of the survey, 62 percent of whom were killed by a militia, 28 percent by unknown persons, and two percent by al-Qaeda in Iraq. Additionally, 57 percent of those surveyed reported fleeing to Syria because of a direct threat to his or her life.[186] The survey also found that 68 percent reported interrogation or harassment by militias or other groups with threats to life, 22 percent had been beaten by militias or other groups, 23 percent had been kidnapped, 72 percent had witnessed a car bombing, and 75 percent had family members, friends, or acquaintances who were killed or murdered."[187] Finally, the survey found that 16 percent reported being tortured.[188] Similarly, IOM has reported that 61 percent of the IDPs it has assessed in Iraq said that they had fled because of a direct threat to their lives and, of these, 85 percent reported being targeted because of their religious or sectarian identity.[189]

Most of the asylum-seekers, refugees and IDPs with whom the Commission met did not believe that security has improved or would improve to such a degree that they would return to Iraq. Many provided specific details about the dangers that remain in their places of origin, including stories of family members who remain in Baghdad being too fearful to travel between different neighborhoods. Furthermore, some reported that their relatives had been killed upon their return. This is consistent with the results of an April Mercy Corps survey of Iraqi refugees in Jordan, in which only 35 percent of the interviewees predicted that they would ever return to Iraq.[190]

Protection and Assistance

In neighboring countries, the initial welcome to Iraqi refugees has worn increasingly thin, and the refugees are now facing stricter border control policies[191] and decreasing resources to support themselves and their families. Refugees fear deportation from or imprisonment in their current countries of asylum, and they are having difficulty supporting themselves and accessing social services. Other than Lebanon, where a sponsorship is required, Iraqi refugees are not permitted to work legally in any of the countries in the region to which they have fled, and many are running out of or have already exhausted the money they brought with them from Iraq. Access to adequate shelter and medical care remain serious problems. Many children do not attend school because their families cannot afford school fees, they are working to help support their families, or their families are fearful of becoming known to authorities and returned to Iraq. There are reports that in order to survive in their countries of asylum, some Iraqi women have turned to prostitution. Host countries also face resource shortages and are finding their basic service sectors overburdened.

While the religiously-based violence that forced many Iraqis to flee has not followed them to their countries of asylum, there have been allegations of religious discrimination against Iraqis in Jordan and Syria. Mandaeans, who do not have an indigenous community in Jordan, report societal discrimination and feel that they need to hide their religious identity there.[192] There also have been reports of Iraqi Shi'a suffering societal discrimination in Jordan, which is a Sunni country with no Shi'a mosques. Several Iraqi Shi'as with whom the Commission met in Amman said that they pretended to be Sunni.[193] UNHCR reported several cases in 2007 of Iraqi Shi'a in Jordan accused of violating a law against "Shi'a proselytization."[194] In Syria, alcohol shops run by Iraqi Christians and Mandaeans reportedly have caused some societal tensions.[195] Reportedly, though, the Syria government has been responsive to concerns raised by the Mandaean community, including allowing Mandaean children in state schools to opt out of mandatory religion classes, which only cover either Christianity or Islam.

Protection also remains a concern for the displaced within Iraq. Security continues to be unstable in some of the areas to which IDPs have fled. In some areas, IDPs have reported forced marriages and evictions, death threats, and being targeted by authorities for arrest and search campaigns, often because they are suspected of being insurgents. Groups of IDPs in some particularly insecure areas have been ordered to return to their places of origin.[196] In addition, in the more religiously-observant regions of Iraq, IDPs have been forced to comply with stricter Islamic customs, including dress codes or prohibitions on girls attending school.[197]

UNHCR and IOM report that 11 of 18 Iraqi governorates have imposed entry requirements for economic and security reasons. Some governorates are allowing residence only to IDPs who can prove they originate from that governorate; others are ordering IDPs to prove they are being sponsored by someone who lives there. Of particular concern is that some governorates, such as Basra and Kirkuk, are registering only IDPs whose family is originally from that area so that the demographics of the governorate will not change.[198]

There are great humanitarian needs for Iraqi IDPs. Access to adequate shelter and health care is of concern, as is access to food and employment. Additionally, IOM reported in 2007 that because of schools being overcrowded, some children joined militias either out of boredom or for money.[199] Refugees International reports that IDPs have joined militias as a result of the security and assistance that these militias provide. The report also describes how militias and other non-state actors have filled the humanitarian void by providing assistance such as settling housing disputes and providing food and other items. Refugees International also reports that many Sunnis allege that the Iraqi Ministry of Displacement and Migration (MoDM) discriminates in favor of displaced Shi'a.[200]

The lack of employment and educational opportunities in their new locations, the fact that the displaced are treated as guests, not refugees, in their countries of asylum, and the high levels of trauma and violence suffered by displaced Iraqis have led to fears that this vulnerable population could become a fertile ground for terrorism or instability in the region.

To address the needs of IDPs and refugees, in February 2008, the Iraqi government announced it would provide $40 million in assistance to IDPs and refugees in neighboring countries, on top of the $25 million it pledged in 2007 to Syria, Jordan, and Lebanon. An Iraqi parliamentary committee on displacement and migration has requested that $4 billion be allotted in the 2009 budget to address the refugee and IDP crisis, although this request has yet to be acted on by the government. Last year, the same committee asked the government to allocate 3 to 5 percent of oil revenues to cover the needs of IDPs and refugees and in the spring it asked for $2 billion for the same purposes; $200 million was allocated.[201]

In July 2008, the Iraqi Ministry of Displacement and Migration announced a national policy on internally displaced persons, which prohibits discrimination against displaced persons, affirms the government's commitment to prevent displacement, confront perpetrators, and protect property left behind, and affirms that IDPs have the right to return to their places of origin, to integrate locally, or to resettle elsewhere in Iraq. This policy is, however, vague in terms of developing concrete programs to address assistance, return, employment, or property restitution.

Returns

Since the end of 2007, a number of Iraqi refugees and IDPs have returned to their previous homes. Nevertheless, refugee advocates, humanitarian organizations, and UNHCR continue to caution against returns, because an adequate system to manage returns has yet to be implemented.

The returns began in November and December 2007, after the Iraqi government announced that it was offering refugees free bus rides from Syria to Baghdad. UNHCR estimated that 45,000 refugees from Syria and 3,700 IDP families returned to Baghdad during this period. According to the MoDM, 3,657 IDP families returned to Baghdad and an additional 6,000 were awaiting registration at year's end.[202] While Iraqi Prime Minister al-Maliki pointed to these returns as evidence of improved security, a UNHCR survey of some returnees from Syria indicated that 46 percent of those surveyed said they were returning because they had exhausted their financial resources, 25 percent because of visa restrictions imposed by Syria in October 2007 at the request of the Iraqi government, and only 14 percent because they felt security in Iraq had improved. The vast majority of returnees settled into neighborhoods or governorates controlled by members of their own religious community. ChaldoAssyrian Christians, Mandaeans, and Yazidis are not believed to have been among these returnees.

Refugee returns have continued in 2008, although not all returnees have been able to resettle in their own homes, leading to secondary displacement. The Iraqi government has chartered flights to return more than 1,000 Iraqis from Egypt.[203] Similar efforts are being undertaken in Jordan, where the Iraqi government has been transporting refugees by bus and plane back to Iraq, and UNHCR Jordan has been providing financial assistance. UNHCR staff monitoring the Iraq-Syria border for 10 days in September reported that 10 to 20 refugee families were returning to Iraq per day. UNHCR plans to recruit additional staff to continue monitoring the border.[204] Reportedly, 800 doctors have returned to Iraq, a population the government of Iraq has been seeking to lure back by offering salaries of $2,000 to $3,000 per month.[205] According to Iraqi television Al Iraqia, 45 Assyrian Christian displaced families returned to their homes in the neighborhood of Dora.[206]

Return numbers of IDPs have been larger than those of refugees. IOM reports that approximately 29,000 IDP families have returned to their areas of origin, but again not necessarily to their homes. However, IOM has also reported that of 151,000 families that had fled Baghdad, fewer than 17,000 had returned by mid-September. The UNHCR reports that between June and October 2008, 140,000 displaced Iraqis have returned to their homes, with High Commissioner Antonio Guterres stating that returns have been facilitated by the Iraqi Security Forces removing squatters from returnees' residences and that, "It is clear that the security situation has improved."[207]

Interviews with some returning refugees indicate that they are returning because of the difficult economic conditions in their countries of asylum. The Iraqi government is providing returning families with cash assistance, but there are concerns about inadequate employment opportunities and services.

In May 2008, Prime Minister al-Maliki announced that the Iraqi government would provide the MoDM with $195 million to promote returns.[208] In August, the government of Iraq announced an effort to identify and remove squatters occupying the homes of refugees and IDPs. Prime Minister Order 101 requires all squatters in Baghdad to vacate houses owned by refugees or IDPs or face prosecution on charges of terrorism. IDP squatters who abide by the order and vacate the property are compensated with 300,000 Iraqi Dinars (about $250) per month for six months.[209] The order also established centers in Baghdad to facilitate returns and calls on the development of a system to replicate the centers countrywide.[210]

Both UNHCR and the U.S. State Department welcomed this announcement, but emphasized that returns should occur only when the security conditions, policy framework, government services, infrastructure, and resources permit. UNCHR's position continues to be that conditions in Iraq do not yet allow for safe, dignified, and sustainable returns.[211]

U.S. Government Policies toward Iraqi Refugees and IDPs

In February 2007, Secretary of State Condoleezza Rice announced that Under Secretary of State for Democracy and Global Affairs Paula Dobriansky would lead an Iraq Refugee and Internally Displaced Persons Task Force to coordinate assistance for refugees and IDPs, as well as U.S. resettlement efforts. In September of that year, the State Department and the Department of Homeland Security announced senior coordinators for Iraqi refugee issues, Ambassador James Foley and Lori Scialabba, to further address the crisis. In fiscal year 2007, the United States contributed approximately $170 million to the various organizations that are assisting Iraqi refugees and IDPs. Its fiscal year 2008, the United States planned to contribute approximately $280 million to UN and non-governmental organizations to meet the needs of Iraqi refugees and internally displaced persons.[212]

In 2007, UNHCR referred more than 20,000 of the most vulnerable Iraqi refugees to third countries for resettlement; half of them were referred to the United States. Although the U.S. government said it planned to resettle 2,000 Iraqis in the United States by the end of September 2007, only 1,600 actually were resettled. This was in addition to 692 Iraqi refugees admitted to the United State from fiscal year 2003 to fiscal year 2006.

In fiscal year 2008, the U.S. government surpassed its goal of resettling 12,000 Iraqis to the United States. The State Department announced in mid-September that it had resettled 12,118 Iraqi refugees, with more than 1,000 booked to travel to the United States before the end of the month. The State Department also announced that the U.S. government expects to be able to admit a minimum of 17,000 Iraqi refugees for resettlement in fiscal year 2009.[213] In May, the U.S. government opened an office in the Green Zone in Baghdad to process and resettle Iraqis who had previously worked for the U.S. government and their families. Department of Homeland Security personnel have started processing the refugees and some are slated to be resettled in the United States.

In February 2008, the State Department announced a new policy increasing direct access for certain Iraqis to the U.S. Refugee Admissions Program, as required by the Refugee Crisis in Iraq Act of 2007.[214] Among the requirements of that Act is the creation of a new P2 priority category for certain Iraqis from "religious or minority" communities with close family members in the United States, allowing them to apply directly for resettlement in the U.S. without first having to be referred by UNHCR.[215] The amendment also authorized the Secretary of State to create additional P2 categories for other vulnerable Iraqis.[216]

The policy announced by the State Department does not expressly refer to any particular community or communities, nor to "religious or minority" communities as the Act stipulated. Instead, it focuses on the close family aspect of the statutory provision. The new category applies to Iraqis in Egypt or Jordan "who are the spouses, sons, daughters, parents, brothers or sisters of a citizen of the United States, or who are the spouses or unmarried sons or daughters of a Permanent Resident Alien of the United States, as established by their being or becoming beneficiaries of approved family-based I-130 Immigrant Visa Petitions." Many of the religious minority asylum seekers, refugees, and IDPs with whom the Commission met in Sweden, Jordan, Syria, and Iraq have family members in the United States, but in most cases, they are extended family or the family members are not yet U.S. citizens or permanent residents; thus, the new P2 category created pursuant to the Act will not apply to them.

Prior Commission Action

The Secretary of State designated Saddam Hussein's Iraq a "country of particular concern" (CPC) under the International Religious Freedom Act (IRFA) from 1999 until 2002. The Commission recommended this status, citing extensive, systematic government violations of religious freedom, and began reporting on Iraq in 2002. The Secretary dropped the CPC designation in 2003, following the U.S. intervention and the subsequent collapse of Saddam Hussein's government. Since that time, the Commission has advocated for religious freedom and universal human rights protections for all persons in Iraq, primarily by calling for constitutional and legal reforms to ensure these rights are guaranteed and enforced in law. The Commission also has reported on other religious freedom issues, noting improvements in some areas but new and continuing problems in others—including the alarming levels of religiously-motivated violence and human rights abuses and the extreme vulnerability of non-Muslims, including ChaldoAssyrian Christians, other Christians, Sabean Mandaeans, and Yazidis.

In April 2003, the Commission urged President Bush to work with Iraqis to ensure that every one of them could exercise his or her equal right to freedom of thought, conscience, religion or belief and related human rights in full accordance with international human rights standards to which Iraq is bound by its ratification of international human rights treaties. In February 2004, the Commission expressed concern to CPA leaders that the initial drafts of Iraq's Transitional Administrative Law (TAL) failed to guarantee the individual right to freedom of thought, conscience, and religion or belief to every Iraqi and that it established Islam as an official source of national legislation, which could be used to justify laws impinging on the right to freedom of expression of all Iraqis, including members of Iraq's Muslim majority, and to discriminate against non-Muslims in a variety of areas. Later that year, the Commission issued recommendations advocating extensive individual human rights protections in Iraq's permanent constitution, and subsequently met with Secretary of State Colin Powell to urge that these recommendations be advocated by the U.S. government and, in turn, implemented by the Iraqi government.

In August 2004, the Commission wrote to U.S. Ambassador to Iraq John Negroponte out of concern over violence targeting religious institutions and leaders, including Shi'a leaders and mosques and churches in Baghdad and Mosul, and urged the U.S. and Iraqi governments to act to prevent further attacks and protect potential victims. In December of that year, in a letter to President Bush, the Commission expressed alarm about rising violence against places of worship, holy sites, and individual believers, particularly from Iraq's non-Muslim minorities, and the increasing flight from the country of members of these groups. The Commission subsequently met with the President and was the first U.S. government body to urge him to ensure that the U.S. government take measures to safeguard and support these minorities by increasing security and channeling U.S. reconstruction and election resources directly to them, as well as by ensuring that the permanent Iraqi constitution would legally protect their rights.

The Commission advocated for similar legal protections for all following the election of Iraq's National Assembly in 2005, urging both Iraqi civil society leaders and U.S. Ambassador Zalmay Khalilzad to promote constitutional guarantees for freedom of thought, conscience, and religion or belief for all Iraqis, including religious minorities and women.[217] In March 2006, in a detailed legal analysis of the newly adopted Iraqi constitution, the Commission expressed concern that constitutional provisions that established Islam as "a foundation source" of legislation,[218] prohibited the passage of laws contrary to "the established provisions of Islam,"[219] and "guarantee[d] the Islamic identity of the majority of the Iraqi people"[220] could result in human rights abuses and discrimination against non-Muslims, non-conforming Muslims, women, and others.

In May 2006, the Commission concluded that the United States' direct involvement in Iraq's political reconstruction created a special obligation to act vigorously, together with the Iraqi leadership, to address the alarming levels of sectarian violence and religiously-motivated human rights abuses taking place in Iraq and to implement the legal, judicial and other institutional reforms necessary to implement human rights protections there. The Commission also warned that the level of violence and abuses, and the resulting flight, of members of Iraq's smallest minorities threatened to end these ancient communities' presence in Iraq. USCIRF recommended a number of security and other measures for immediate adoption.

During 2006, Commissioners met with senior U.S. and Iraqi officials, including Iraqi ministers and representatives of the U.S. National Security Council, as well as experts from the Iraq Study Group, Iraqi human rights activists, legal experts, and representatives of Iraq's diverse religious communities, to stress that international human rights standards must be understood to protect each Iraqi as an individual, not just as a member of a particular ethnic, political, or religious group. During a mission to Turkey in 2006, the Commission met with Christian religious leaders to investigate the situation of Iraqi Christian refugees who had sought refuge in that country. In December 2006, the Commission expressed its disappointment that the Iraq Study Group's report did not incorporate human rights promotion as part of the way forward for U.S. policy in Iraq. The Commission emphasized that "[h]uman rights protections and accountability for abuses will serve to address past abuses under Saddam Hussein and ongoing abuses that have arisen in the form of death squads and other unlawful violence. Without an effective system that can account for these and other human rights violations, instability will persist." The Commission also recommended a senior official be placed at Embassy Baghdad to address human rights violations in Iraq.

In May 2007, the Commission placed Iraq on its Watch List, citing escalating unchecked sectarian violence, mounting evidence of collusion between Shi'a militias and Iraqi government ministries, and the grave conditions affecting the country's smallest religious minorities.[221] In a subsequent May 2007 meeting with, and September 2007 letter to, Secretary of State Rice, the Commission urged U.S. action to address the severe threats to these minorities, including through security, humanitarian, development, and reconciliation measures. Among other recommendations, the Commission proposed that the State Department convene urgent meetings both inside and outside Iraq, bringing together representatives of Iraq's non-Muslim minorities to hear directly from them what the U.S. and Iraqi governments could do to protect their communities.

The Commission repeatedly called attention to the dire plight of Iraqi refugees and IDPs and urged the U.S. government both to increase humanitarian assistance and to expand and expedite its refugee and asylum programs for Iraqis fleeing religious persecution, particularly those from Iraq's smallest religious groups. Since 2004, the Commission has sent letters on this topic to President Bush, Secretary of State Rice, Under Secretary of State Dobriansky, and others, and met with senior administration officials and members of Congress. In December 2006, the Commission published an op-ed on the subject in *The Washington Times*,[222] which helped spur congressional hearings and led the State Department, in February 2007, to establish the task force on Iraqi refugees as described previously. The Commission's 2007 annual report included a number of other specific policy recommendations in this area.

Since 2007, the Commission has advocated for the creation of Priority 2 (P2) category in the U.S. Refugee Admission Program to allow Iraq's smallest, most vulnerable religious minorities, including ChaldoAssyrian Christians, Sabean Mandaeans, and Yazidis, direct access to the program without having to be referred by UNHCR. In February 2008, the State Department announced a new policy increasing direct access to the program for Iraqis, although only for Iraqi refugees in Egypt or Jordan who are close family members of a U.S. citizen or permanent resident. The Commission continues to urge that members of Iraq's smallest religious minorities be allowed to apply directly to the U.S. Refugee Admissions Program, and that family unification options for these particularly vulnerable refugees with relatives in the United States should be expanded to include extended family.

Recommendations for U.S. Policy

Commissioners unanimously agree that the religious freedom situation in Iraq is dire, and concur on the following recommendations to advance human rights protections for all Iraqis, including the freedom of thought, conscience, and religion or belief, and to address the plight of Iraq's most vulnerable and smallest religious minorities.

I.   Ensuring Safe and Fair Elections

To ensure that upcoming provincial elections are safe, fair, and free of intimidation and violence, the U.S. government should:

- lead an international effort to protect voters and voting places and to monitor the elections;

- direct U.S. military and coalition forces, where feasible and appropriate, to provide heightened security for the elections, particularly in minority areas, such as in Nineveh governorate, where there were irregularities in previous elections; and

- urge the Iraqi government at the highest levels to ensure security and to permit and facilitate election monitoring by experts from local and international NGOs, the international community, and the United Nations, particularly in minority areas, such as in Nineveh governorate, where there were irregularities in previous elections.

II.   Ensuring Security and Safety for all Iraqis

To protect the security and human rights of all members of religious communities, particularly vulnerable religious minorities such as ChaldoAssyrian Christians, Sabean Mandaeans and Yazidis, the U.S. government should urge the Iraqi government at the highest levels to:

- urgently establish, fund, train, and deploy police units for vulnerable minority communities that are as representative as possible of those communities, ensure that minority police recruits are not excluded from nor discriminated against in the recruitment process, in promotion and command leadership opportunities, or in the terms and conditions of their employment, and ensure to the maximum extent possible that such police units remain in their locations of origin and are not transferred to other cities as has been done in the past;

- continue efforts to ensure that new national identification cards do not list religious or ethnic identity, and expedite the development and issuance of such cards; and

- take steps to enhance security at places of worship, particularly in areas where religious minorities are known to be at risk.

To eliminate remaining sectarianism in the Iraqi government and security forces and reduce sectarian violence and human rights abuses, the U.S. government should urge the Iraqi government at the highest levels to:

- ensure that Iraqi government revenues neither are directed to nor indirectly support any militia, para-state actor, or other organization credibly charged with involvement in severe human rights abuses;

- suspend immediately any government personnel charged with engagement in sectarian violence and other human rights abuses, undertake transparent and effective investigations of such charges, and bring the perpetrators to justice; and

- continue the process of ensuring a greater sectarian integration into the government and security forces so that they better reflect the diversity of the country.

III. Making Prevention of Abuses against Religious Minorities a High Priority

To address the severe abuses against Iraq's most vulnerable and smallest religious minorities, the U.S. government should urge the Iraqi government at the highest levels to:

- replace the existing Prime Minister's minorities committee with one that is independent and includes representatives of all of Iraq's ethnic and religious minority communities who are selected by the communities themselves, and ensure that this committee has access for communicating minority concerns to senior officials of the Iraqi government and the international community;

- work with minority communities and their representatives to develop measures to implement Article 125 of the Iraqi Constitution, which guarantees "the administrative, political, cultural, and educational rights of the various nationalities, such as Turkomen, Chaldeans, Assyrians, and all the other constituents," in Nineveh and other areas where these groups are concentrated;

- direct the Ministry of Human Rights to investigate and issue a public report on abuses against and the marginalization of Iraq's minority communities and making recommendations to address such abuses;

- make public the results of the Iraqi government's reported investigation into the recent attacks against Christians in Mosul when that investigation is completed, and bring the perpetrators of those attacks to justice; and

- enact constitutional amendments to strengthen human rights guarantees in the Iraqi Constitution, including by:

  --clarifying sub-clause (B) in Article 2 that no law may contradict "the rights and basic freedoms stipulated in this constitution" to make clear that these rights and freedoms include the principles of equality and nondiscrimination and the human rights guaranteed under international agreements to which Iraq is a State party;

--deleting sub-clause (A) in Article 2 that no law may contradict "the established provisions of Islam," because it heightens sectarian tensions over which interpretation of Islam prevails and improperly makes theological interpretations into constitutional questions

--revising Article 2's guarantee of "the Islamic identity of the majority" to make certain that this identity is not used to justify violations of the individual right to freedom of thought, conscience, religion or belief under international law;

--ensuring that minority identity is also guaranteed, including the rights of all individual members of ethnic, religious or linguistic minorities to enjoy and develop their culture and language and to practice their religion;

--making clear that the default system for personal status cases in Iraq is civil law, that the free and informed consent of both parties is required to move a personal status case to the religious law system, that religious court rulings are subject to final review under Iraq's civil law, and that the appointment of judges to courts adjudicating personal status matters, including any religious courts, should meet international standards with respect to judicial training; and

--removing the ability of making appointments to the Federal Supreme Court based on training in Islamic jurisprudence alone, and requiring that, at a minimum, all judges must have training in civil law, including a law degree.

In addition, the U.S. government should:

- immediately revive the U.S. government's internal Inter-Agency Task Force on Iraqi minority issues and direct it to consider and recommend policies for the U.S. government to implement to address the needs of these vulnerable communities; and

- facilitate a series of conferences, both inside and outside Iraq, bringing together representatives of Iraq's smallest religious minorities to allow them to discuss and help them come to consensus on recommendations to the U.S. and Iraqi governments on measures to protect their communities.

IV.   Ensuring that the Kurdistan Regional Government Upholds Minority Rights

To address the marginalization of religious and ethnic minorities in northern Iraq, including in disputed areas, the U.S. government should:

- press the Kurdistan Regional Government (KRG) and Kurdish officials in neighboring governorates to cease alleged interference with the creation, training, and deployment of representative police forces for minority communities, and link progress on representative policing to U.S. financial assistance and other forms of interaction with the KRG;

- demand immediate investigations into and accounting for allegations of human rights abuses by Kurdish regional and local officials against minority communities, including reports of attacks on minorities and expropriation of minority property, and make clear that decisions on U.S. financial and other assistance will take into account whether perpetrators are being investigated and held accountable; and

- work with Iraqi and KRG officials to establish a mechanism to examine and resolve outstanding real property claims involving religious and ethnic minorities in the KRG region and neighboring governorates.

V.   Re-Focusing U.S. Financial Assistance

To address the marginalization of religious and ethnic minorities in northern Iraq, including in disputed areas, the U.S. government should:

- direct U.S. assistance funds to projects that develop the political ability of ethnic and religious minorities to organize themselves and effectively convey their concerns to the government;

- declare and establish a fair allocation of U.S. foreign assistance funding for ChaldoAssyrian Christian, Sabean Mandaean, Yazidi, and other small religious and ethnic minority communities, ensure that the use of these funds is determined by independent minority national and town representatives, and establish direct lines of communication between such independent structures and U.S. Provincial Reconstruction Team Nineveh, separate from the Iraqi government and the Kurdistan Regional Government, in order to ensure that U.S. assistance fairly benefits all religious and ethnic minority groups and is not being withheld by local and regional government officials; and

- require that the Government Accountability Office, the Special Inspector General for Iraq Reconstruction, or another appropriate entity conduct an independent audit of past and current U.S. and Iraqi government reconstruction and development assistance to religious and ethnic minority areas and provide recommendations for future assistance.

To eliminate remaining sectarianism in the Iraqi government and security forces and reduce sectarian violence and human rights abuses, the U.S. government should:

- ensure that U.S. foreign assistance and security assistance programs do not directly or indirectly provide financial, material or other benefits to (1) government security units and/or para-governmental militias responsible for severe human rights abuses or otherwise engaged in sectarian violence; or (2) political parties or other organizations that advocate or condone policies at odds with Iraq's international human rights obligations, or whose aims include the destruction or undermining of such international human rights guarantees; and

- fund programs to educate and train Ministry of Interior and Ministry of Defense personnel on international human rights standards, particularly as they relate to religious freedom.

To advance human rights protections for all Iraqis, the U.S. government should:

- fund capacity-building programs for the Iraqi Ministry of Human Rights, the independent national Human Rights Commission, and a new independent minorities committee whose membership is selected by the communities;

- fund the deployment of a group of human rights experts to consult with the Iraqi Council of Representatives and the constitutional amendment committee and to assist with legal drafting and implementation matters related to strengthening human rights provisions, including freedom of thought, conscience, and religion or belief;

- fund workshops and training sessions on religion/state issues for Iraqi officials, policymakers, legal professionals, representatives of non-governmental organizations (NGOs), religious leaders, and other members of key sectors of society; and

- expand the Iraqi visitors program through the State Department to focus on exchange and educational opportunities in the United States related to freedom of religion and religious tolerance for Iraqi officials, policymakers, legal professionals, representatives of NGOs, religious leaders, and other members of key sectors of society.

VI.   Addressing Religious Extremism

To address concerns of religious extremism in Iraq, the U.S. government should:

- continue to speak out at the highest levels to condemn religiously-motivated violence by both Shi'a and Sunni groups, including violence targeting women and members of religious minorities, as well as efforts by local officials and extremist groups to enforce religious law in violation of the Iraqi Constitution and international human rights standards;

- urge the Iraqi government at the highest levels to locate and close illegal courts unlawfully imposing extremist interpretations of Islamic law;

- give clear directives to U.S. officials and recipients of U.S. democracy-building grants to assign greater priority to projects that promote multi-religious and multi-ethnic efforts to encourage religious tolerance and understanding, that foster knowledge of and respect for universal human rights standards, and that build judicial capacity to foster the rule of law; and

- fund civic education programs in schools that teach religious tolerance and the historical nature of Iraq as a multi-religious and multi-ethnic state.

VII. Promoting Respect for Human Rights

To address past and current reports of human rights violations in Iraq, the U.S. government should:

- appoint and immediately dispatch a Special Envoy for Human Rights in Iraq to Embassy Baghdad, reporting directly to the Secretary of State, to serve as the United States' lead human rights official in Iraq, to lead an Embassy human rights working group, including the senior coordinators on Article 140 issues, on corruption, and on the rule of law, as well as other relevant officials including those focusing on minority issues, and to coordinate U.S. efforts to promote and protect human rights in Iraq; and

- appoint immediately one or more U.S. advisors under the Department of State's Iraq Reconstruction Management Office to serve as liaisons to the Iraqi Ministry of Human Rights.

To address past and current reports of human rights violations in Iraq, the U.S. government should urge the Iraqi government at the highest levels to:

- undertake transparent and effective investigations of human rights abuses, including those stemming from sectarian, religiously-motivated, or other violence by Iraqi security forces, political factions, militias or any other para-state actors affiliated with or otherwise linked to the Iraqi government or regional or local governments, and bring the perpetrators to justice;

- cooperate with international investigations of such abuses, and

- create and fully fund the independent national Human Rights Commission provided for in the Iraqi Constitution and ensure that this Commission is non-sectarian, that it has a mandate to investigate individual complaints, and that its functions and operations are based on the UN's Paris Principles.

To respond to reports of the confiscation of houses of worship, the U.S. government should urge the Iraqi government at the highest levels to

- promptly terminate any seizures and conversions of places of worship and other religious properties and restore previously seized and converted properties to their rightful owners and provide appropriate compensation.

VIII.   Addressing the Situation of Internally Displaced Persons and Refugees

To address the humanitarian needs of Iraqi internally displaced persons (IDPs) and refugees, the U.S. government should

- fund a much larger proportion of all UN appeals for humanitarian assistance to Iraqi IDPs and refugees;

- urge the Iraqi government to fund a much larger proportion of all UN appeals for humanitarian assistance to Iraqis and to increase its own assistance to IDPs;

- utilize diplomatic efforts to urge U.S. allies in Iraq to increase humanitarian assistance to, and resettlement opportunities for, vulnerable Iraqi refugees and IDPs;

- increase assistance to humanitarian organizations, host nations, and host communities that are providing necessary aid to vulnerable Iraqi IDPs and refugees; funded assistance programs should provide medical care for basic, advanced and chronic medical concerns, including prescription drugs; psychosocial care for victims of trauma; formal, informal, and non-formal education opportunities; direct financial assistance to alleviate the high costs of shelter; packages to provide for basic needs, including increased food distribution programs; and information campaigns;

- fund capacity-building programs for the Iraqi Ministry of Displacement and Migration to ensure that it can adequately provide assistance and protection to internally displaced persons;

- provide assistance from and guidance by the U.S. Agency for International Development to the government of Iraq to reform the Public Distribution System so that displaced Iraqis can register for and receive food rations in their new location;

- work to ensure that no assistance is provided to IDPs by political factions, militias, or any other actor implicated in sectarian violence or other human rights abuses; and

- encourage countries to which Iraqis have fled, in particular Jordan and Syria, to allow refugees to work;

To ensure freedom of movement for Iraqis fleeing religious or other persecution, the U.S. government should

- encourage neighboring countries, in particular Jordan and Syria, to reform border policies to enable vulnerable refugees to enter; and

- encourage Iraqi governorates to remove entry restrictions and registration policies that limit the ability of vulnerable Iraqis to enter.

To address the increasing incidents of returns or attempted returns by IDPs and refugees to their locations of origin, the U.S. government should

- clearly state that the U.S. government does not encourage the premature return of Iraqi refugees to Iraq until necessary conditions are met, including security, assistance, legal frameworks, and integration programs;

- encourage and fund information campaigns, including "go and see visits" by religious and/or community leaders selected by the refugees/IDPs to ensure that displaced Iraqis considering return have the proper information needed to make informed decisions;

- work with the government of Iraq and international organizations to help the government of Iraq develop the legal framework necessary to address property disputes resulting when displaced Iraqis attempt to return to homes that have been occupied by others or destroyed, and stop the efforts of sectarian militias to resolve such property disputes on their own; and

- increase the capacity of assistance organizations to provide long-term assistance, including shelter, food, and other essential services, to returning Iraqis.

To facilitate the resettlement to the United States of the most vulnerable Iraqis, the U.S. government should

- amend the U.S. Refugee Admissions Program's new P2 category to allow Iraq's smallest, most vulnerable religious minorities direct access to the program; in addition, family reunification should be expanded for these refugees with relatives in the United States to include not only immediate family members, but as has been done in prior refugee crisis situations, to also include extended family such as grandparents, aunts and uncles, cousins, etc.;

- ensure that members of Iraq's smallest, most vulnerable religious minorities scheduled to be resettled to the United States are not delayed unnecessarily by (1) providing adequate personnel to conduct background screening procedures, and (2) enforcing proper application of the existing waiver of the material support bar to those forced to provide support to terrorists under duress;

- enhance the resettlement processing capabilities of the Department of Homeland Security by increasing the number of interviewing officers and allowing State Department officials to conduct interviews in order to keep pace with referrals from the UN High Commissioner for Refugees (UNHCR) and meet the statutorily-permitted maximum of admissions for the region; and

- continue to raise with UNHCR any reports of discrimination by local employees against religious minority refugees in the resettlement process.

---

[1] Congressional Record, S12999, November 12, 1998.
[2] "President's Statement on Failure of the Senate Procedural Motion," the White House, February 17, 2007.
[3] Anthony H. Cordesman, *Iraqi Force Development and the Challenge of Civil War*, Testimony before the Committee on Armed Services, U.S. House of Representatives, March 28, 2007; Barry R. McCaffrey, *After Action Report, Visit to Iraq and Kuwait 9 – 16 March 2007*, March 26, 2007, pg. 3.

[4] The Commission was scheduled to travel to Baghdad in late October 2008, but the trip was postponed by the U.S. Embassy because it was moving into a new building. In place of the trip, the Department of State kindly facilitated a number of videoconferences with officials and individuals in Baghdad.

[5] "Iraq," *Annual Report 2007*, U.S. Commission on International Religious Freedom, May 2007.

[6] *See., e.g.,* Stephen Biddle, Michael E. O'Hanlon, and Kenneth M. Pollack, "How to Leave a Stable Iraq," *Foreign Affairs*, September/October 2008; *Measuring Stability and Security in Iraq,* U.S. Department of Defense, September 26, 2008; Bob Woodward, *The War Within: A Secret White House History 2006- 2008* (Simon & Schuster 2008); *Securing, Stabilizing, and Rebuilding Iraq: Progress Report: Some Gains Made, Updated Strategy Needed,* U.S. Government Accountability Office, June 23, 2008; *Iraq after the Surge I & II,* International Crisis Group, April 2008; Glenn Kessler, "When the Data Don't Really Measure Up," *The Washington Post*, April 9, 2008 (quoting 2007 National Intelligence Estimate); "Iraq," *Country Reports on Human Rights Practices 2007*, U.S. Department of State, March 2008.

[7] *Measuring Stability and Security in Iraq,* U.S. Department of Defense, September 26, 2008.

[8] The ongoing dispute between Kurds, Arabs, and Turkomen over the status of Kirkuk and nearby areas has led to increased tensions, and even some violence, in 2008. In July in Kirkuk, a suicide bomber detonated explosives in a crowd of Kurds protesting the draft provincial election law, killing at least 24 and wounding 187. Many Kurds believed that Turkomen were behind the attack and retaliated by storming and vandalizing the offices of the Turkomen political parties in the city. In late August/early September, there was a tense standoff between Kurdish *peshmerga* forces and Iraqi government forces over control of the town of Khanaquin, although the dispute was ultimately resolved peacefully, with both sides agreeing to stay outside of the town and allow security to be provided by the local police.

[9] Tim Cocks, "Militants will try to disrupt election: UN," *Reuters*, November 30, 2008; *Report of the Secretary-General to the Security Council pursuant to paragraph 6 of resolution 1830 (2008)*, United Nations Document S/2008/688, November 6, 2008, para. 55; Secretary of Defense Robert M. Gates, Testimony before the House Armed Services Committee, "Security and Stability in Afghanistan and Iraq," September 10, 2008.

[10] "Iraq civilian, U.S. troop deaths fall in September," *Reuters*, October 1, 2008.

[11] "Death toll down for U.S. troops, Iraqi civilians in October," *CNN*, October 31, 2008; "Dozens killed in Iraqi bombings," *BBC*, December 2, 2008.

[12] "Iraq," *Country Reports on Human Rights Practice 2005*, U.S. Department of State, March 2006; see also Kenneth Timmerman, "Christians Want Police Protection in Iraq," *NewsMax*, April 28, 2008.

[13] "Iraq," *International Religious Freedom Report 2008*, U.S. State Department, September 2008.

[14] Simon Caldwell, "Bishop Asks: Is it the 'End of Christianity in Iraq?'" *Catholic News Service*, December 1, 2007.

[15] "Christians trickling back to their homes in Mosul," *IRIN News* November 6, 2008.

[16] "UNHCR aiding uprooted Iraqi Christians," UN High Commissioner for Refugees, October 24, 2008.

[17] "Christians Trickling Back to Mosul," *IRIN News* November 6, 2008.

[18] Gary Max "In Mosul, a Battle for Christians," *Chicago Tribune,* November 24, 2008.

[19] *Human Rights Report, 1 January – 30 June 2008*, UN Assistance Mission in Iraq, December 2008, pg. 17.

[20] Ibid., pg. 10.

[21] Albert Michael, "Islamic Group Sends Threatening Letter to Churches in North Iraq," *Assyrian International News Agency*, July 2, 2008.

[22] "Two Christians Kidnapped and Killed in Mosul," *AsiaNews,* September 2, 2008.

[23] "Church Bombings in Iraq Since 2004," *Assyrian International News Agency,* July 1, 2008

[24] Preti Taneja, *Assimilation, Exodus, Eradication: Iraq's Minority Communities Since 2003*, Minority Rights Groups International, 2007, pg. 9.

[25] Ibid., pg. 9

[26] John Pontifex, "Religious Cleansing in Iraq," *ACN News*, January 9, 2008.

[27] "Vicar: Dire Times for Iraq's Christians," *60 Minutes*, December 2, 2007.

[28] Aseel Kami "Iraq cardinal: Christians not singled out for attack," *Reuters* January 8, 2008.

[29] Testimony of Pascale Warda, Hearing on "Threats to Iraq's Communities of Antiquity," U.S. Commission on International Religious Freedom, July 25, 2007.

[30] *Human Rights Report, 1 September – 31 October 2006* UN Assistance Mission in Iraq, November 2006, pg. 13

[31] Sholnn Freeman, "Iraqi Christians Struggle With Fear After Slayings," *The Washington Post*, April 22, 2008.

[32] Testimony of Rev. Canon White, Hearing on "Threats to Iraq's Communities of Antiquity," U.S. Commission on International Religious Freedom, July 25, 2007.

[33] Testimony of Robert Carey, Vice President of Resettlement and Chairman, Refugee Council USA, International Rescue Committee, before the Congressional Caucus for Religious Minorities in the Middle East, April 18, 2008.

[34] Interviews with Iraqi Christian refugees in Sodertalje, Sweden on November 12, 2007, in Amman, Jordan on March 8, 2008 and March 10, 2008 and with Iraqi Christian IDPs in Erbil, Iraq on March 12, 2008.

[35] "Iraq," *International Religious Freedom Report 2008*, U.S. State Department, September 2008.

[36] "Iraq," *International Religious Freedom Report 2006*, U.S. State Department, September 2006.

[37] Interviews with Iraqi Christian refugees in Sodertalje, Sweden on November 12, 2007 and in Amman, Jordan on March 10 and 12, 2008.

[38] *Escaping Mayhem and Murder, Iraqi Refugees in the Middle East,* U.S. Conference of Catholic Bishops, July 2007, pg. 3

[39] "Vicar: Dire Times for Iraq's Christians," *60 Minutes*, December 2, 2007.; See also Paul Isaac, "The Assault on Assyrian Christians," *International Herald Tribune*, May 8, 2007.

[40] *Human Rights Report, 1 April – 30 June 2007*, UN Assistance Mission for Iraq, October 2007, pg. 8.

[41] Testimony of Rev. Canon Andrew White, Hearing on "Threats to Iraq's Communities of Antiquity," U.S. Commission on International Religious Freedom, July 25, 2007.

[42] Testimony of Donny George, Hearing on "Threats to Iraq's Communities of Antiquity," U.S. Commission on International Religious Freedom, July 25, 2007.

[43] Elena Becatoros **"Iraqis Crowd Churches for Christmas Mass"** *Associated Press* December 27, 2007

[44] "Iraq," *International Religious Freedom Report 2007*, U.S. State Department, September 2008.

[45] "Al-Maliki Vows to Protect Iraqi Christians," *Reuters,* October 12, 2008; Tracy Wilkinson and Ned Parker, "Push Christians to Return, Maliki tells Pope," *Los Angeles Times,* July 26, 2008; "Iraq Weekly Status Report," U.S. Department of State, May 21, 2008, pg. 4 (reporting al-Maliki's pledges to Christians at a meeting in Mosul); "Iraq Working to Ensure Safety of Christians," *Agence France Presse*, January 8, 2008; "Iraqi PM Pledges to Protect Christians," *The Washington Post,* October 29, 2007.

[46] "Iraq: Ransom Deadline for Archbishop Today," *Compass Direct*, March 6, 2008; Cameron W. Barr, "Kidnapped Archbishop Found Dead in Iraq," *The Washington Post,* March 14, 2008.

[47] "Church opposes Iraq death penalty for archbishop's killer" *Agence France Presse* May 19, 2008.

[48] "Iraq," *International Religious Freedom Report 2008*, U.S. State Department, September 2008.

[49] In terms of deaths, according to the report, the Shabak community suffered 529 fatalities during this time period; the Yazidi community, 335; the Christian community, 172; and the Mandaean community, 127. (It should be noted, however, that other accounts conflict with these statistics. For example, the U.S. military has reported that 796 civilians were killed in the August 14, 2007 truck bombings of the northern Yazidi villages of Qahtaniya and Jazeera alone.) In terms of internal displacement, the report states that 3,078 Shabak families, 1,752 Christian families, and 62 Mandaean families are displaced within Iraq. The report did not give internal displacement numbers for Yazidis.

[50] Meeting with Mandaean spiritual leader Sheikh Ganzabra Sattar Jabbar Al-Hilo al-Zahrony, Washington, DC, November 15, 2007

[51] "Iraq," *International Religious Freedom Report 2008*, U.S. State Department, September 2008.

[52] Ashraf al-Khalidi, Sophia Hoffman, and Victor Tanner *Iraqi Refugees in the Syrian Arab Republic: A Field-Based Snapshot* The Brookings Institution—University of Bern Project on Internal Displacement, June 2007, pg. 14.

[53] Interviews with Iraqi Mandaean refugees in Lund, Sweden on November 13, 2007, in Amman, Jordan on March 8, 2008 and in Damascus, Syria on May 20, 2008.

[54] *Mandaean Human Rights Annual Report* Mandaean Human Rights Group, March 2008, pgs. 13-36.

[55] Idib., pg. 7.

[56] Testimony of Mr. Suhaib Nashi, Hearing on "Threats to Iraq's Communities of Antiquity," U.S. Commission on International Religious Freedom, July 25, 2007.

[57] Preti Taneja, *Assimilation, Exodus, Eradication: Iraq's Minority Communities Since 2003*, Minority Rights Groups International, 2007, pg. 12.

[58] Interviews with Iraqi Mandaean refugees in Amman, Jordan on March 8, 2008.

[59] Meeting with Mandaean spiritual leader Sheikh Ganzabra Sattar Jabbar Al-Hilo al-Zahrony, Washington, DC, November 15, 2007.

[60] Preti Taneja, *Assimilation, Exodus, Eradication: Iraq's Minority Communities Since 2003*, Minority Rights Groups International, 2007, pg. 12.

[61] "Iraq," *International Religious Freedom Report 2008*, U.S. State Department, September 2008.

[62] Interviews with Iraqi Mandaean refugees in Damascus, Syria on May 20, 2008.

[63] Meeting with Mandaean spiritual leader Sheikh Ganzabra Sattar Jabbar Al-Hilo al-Zahrony, Washington, DC, November 15, 2007

[64] Ibid.; Interviews with Iraqi Mandaean refugees in Lund, Sweden on November 13, 2007, in Amman, Jordan on March 8, 2008 and in Damascus, Syria on May 20, 2008.

[65] Preti Taneja, *Assimilation, Exodus, Eradication: Iraq's Minority Communities Since 2003*, Minority Rights Groups International, 2007, pg. 13; see also Sebastian Maisel "Social Change Amidst Terror and Discrimination: Yezidis in the New Iraq" *Policy Brief* Middle East Institute, August 2008, pg. 3.

[66] Preti Taneja, *Assimilation, Exodus, Eradication: Iraq's Minority Communities Since 2003*, Minority Rights Groups International, 2007, pg. 13.

[67] Ibid., pg. 13

[68] Ibid., pg. 13

[69] Ibid., pg. 13

[70] Sebastian Maisel "Social Change Amidst Terror and Discrimination: Yezidis in the New Iraq" *Policy Brief* The Middle East Institute, August 2008, pg. 4.

[71] Alissa J. Rubin, "Persecuted Sect in Iraq Avoids Shrine," *The New York Times*, October 14, 2007.

[72] Interviews with Iraqi Yazidi refugees in Damascus, Syria on May 20, 2008.

[73] *"Love and Hate in Iraq, 23 Members Of Yazidi Sect Killed After Woman Who Converted To Islam Was Stoned,"* CBS News, *April 22, 2007.*

[74] Interviews with Iraqi Yazidi refugees in Damascus, Syria on May 20, 2008.

[75] Sebastian Maisel "Social Change Amidst Terror and Discrimination: Yezidis in the New Iraq" *Policy Brief* Middle East Institute, August 2008, executive summary.

[76] "Minority Targeted in Iraq Bombing," *BBC*, August 15, 2007.

[77] *Human Rights Report, 1 January-30 June 2008* UN Assistance Mission in Iraq, December 2008, pg. 17.

[78] Katherine Zoepf and Atheer Kakan, "U.S. Prosecutor goes to Iraq to work on Blackwater case," *The New York Times*, December 7, 2008.

[79] "Yazidis Targeted in Iraq Attack" *BBC News* December 15, 2008; "Seven Yazidis killed in Iraq attack" *Agence France Presse* December 15, 2008.

[80] *State of the World's Minorities 2008; Events of 2007*, Minority Rights Groups International, pg. 151.

[81] Interviews with Iraqi Yazidi refugees in Damascus, Syria on May 20, 2008.

[82] Stephen Farrell "Iraq Bomber Aimed at Alcohol Sellers," *The New York Times*, December 21, 2007.

[83] Meeting with Yazidi representatives in Erbil, Iraq, March 13, 2008.

[84] Alissa J. Rubin, "Persecuted Sect in Iraq Avoids Shrine," *The New York Times*, October 14, 2007.

[85] Sebastian Maisel, "Social Change Amidst Terror and Discrimination: Yezidis in the New Iraq" The Middle East Institute *Policy Brief* August 2008, pg. 5.

[86] "Iraq," *International Religious Freedom Report 2007*, U.S. State Department, September 2007.

[87] "Iraq," *International Religious Freedom Report 2008*, U.S. State Department, September 2008.

[88] "Iraq," *Country Reports on Human Rights Practices 2007*, U.S. State Department, March 2008

[89] The law prohibits travel to the "enemy states" of Israel, Iran, and the United States.

[90] "Iraqi courts acquits legislator for making trip to Israel," *Reuters,* November 24, 2008.

[91] *Quarterly Report* Special Inspector General for Iraqi Reconstruction, October 30, 2008, pg. 98.

[92] "Governorate Profiles: Kirkuik, Ninewa, Salah Al-Din,*"* International Organization for Migration, June 2008, pg. 3 and "Governorate Profiles: Dahuk, Erbil, Sulaymaniyah," International Organization for Migration, June 2008, pg. 3.

[93] Kenneth R. Timmerman, "Kurds Provide Safe Haven for Christians," *NewsMax*, April 24, 2008.

[94] Meeting with KRG Minister of Interior Karim Sinjari, March 13, 3008; Arab Muslim IDPs are viewed by KRG authorities with suspicion and as a security threat and they must secure two local sponsors before entry. Although the Mandaean community is not indigenous to Northern Iraq, a number of Mandaean IDPs have been admitted, and the KRG continues to admit Mandaeans who are vouched for by community members who are already there.

[95] Meeting with Mandaean representative, Erbil, Iraq, March 12, 2008.

[96] Meeting with Yazidi representatives in Erbil, Iraq, March 12, 2008.

[97] Mark Kukis "Is Mosul on the Mend?" *Time* March 7, 2008.

[98] "Measuring Stability and Security in Iraq," Department of Defense, September 2008, pg. 27.

[99] *Quarterly Report* Special Inspector General for Iraqi Reconstruction, October 30, 2008 pg. 92.

[100] "Oil for Soil: Toward a Grand Bargain on Iraq and the Kurds" International Crisis Group, October 28, 2008, pg. 1.

[101] The date of the referendum was to be December 31, 2007, however, resolution of the disputed areas has been delayed due to political disputes.

[102] *Report of the Secretary-General pursuant to paragraph 6 of resolution 1830 (2008),* UN Security Council, November 6, 2008, pg. 11.

[103] Ibid., see also *Human Rights Report, 1 January – 30 June 2008,* UN Assistance Mission in Iraq, December 2008, pg. 17.

[104] The UN proposed that Christians should get three seats on each of these three councils, but the amendment that was adopted gave Christians only one seat on each. The UN also proposed that Yazidis should get three seats on the Nineveh council, but the amendment provided for only one. In addition, Shabaks were allotted one seat in Nineveh and Mandaeans one seat in Baghdad, as the UN proposed.

[105] Tina Susman, "Iraq OKs provincial council quotas for minorities" *Los Angeles Times* November 4, 2008.

[106] Meetings in Erbil, Iraq, March 14, 2008; See also Kenneth Timmerman, "Christians Want Police Protection in Iraq," *NewsMax*, April 28, 2008.

[107] Chaldean Assyrian Syriac Council of America, Preliminary Report on Fact-Finding Trip to Iraq, March 10-20, 2008, pg. 3.

[108] Meeting with KRG Minister of Interior Karim Sinjar in Erbil, Iraq, March 13, 2008.

[109] U.S. Department of State, "Iraq," *Country Reports on Human Rights Practices, 2007,* March 2008.

[110] Fred Aprim, "Kurdish Official Denies Turkomen, Assyrian Land Claims," *Assyrian International News Agency,* March 11, 2007.

[111] Testimony of Michael Youash, Hearing on "Threats to Iraq's Communities of Antiquity." U.S. Commission on International Religious Freedom, July 25, 2007.

[112] Meeting with KRG Minister of Human Rights Yousif Mohammed Aziz in Erbil, Iraq, March 12, 2008.

[113] Meeting with KRG Minister of Finance Sarkis Aghajan Mamendu in Erbil, Iraq, March 12, 2008.

[114] Sebastian Maisel "Social Change Amidst Terror and Discrimination: Yezidis in the New Iraq" *Policy Brief* The Middle East Institute August 2008 pg. 5.

[115] There is a dispute within the Yazidi community as to whether Yazidis are ethnically Yazidi or Kurd. The community also disputes whether Yazidis would be more secure under the protection of the Kurdish or the central government.

[116] *Human Rights Report, 1 January – 30 June 2008,* UN Assistance Mission in Iraq, December 2, 2008, pg. 17.

[117] "Money, Unspent, in Iraq's Pockets" *The New York Times,* October 30, 2008.

[118] *Quarterly Report* Special Inspector General for Iraqi Reconstruction, October 30, 2008, pg. 99.

[119] Testimony of Michael Youash, Hearing on "Threats to Iraq's Communities of Antiquity," U.S. Commission on International Religious Freedom, July 25, 2007.

[120] Christian Solidarity International, *Iraq Christians Face Extinction,* 2007, pg. 12. See also Testimony of Michael Youash, Hearing on "Threats to Iraq's Communities of Antiquity," U.S. Commission on International Religious Freedom, July 25, 2007.

[121] Sebastian Maisel "Social Change Amidst Terror and Discrimination: Yezidis in the New Iraq" *Policy Brief* The Middle East Institute August 2008 pg. 5.

[122] Al-Sadr's faction assumed control of the Agriculture, Health, and Transportation Ministries following the 2005 parliamentary elections—a situation providing ample opportunity to fund and equip Mahdi Army personnel under the auspices of government employment. *The Iraq Study Group Report*, U.S. Institute of Peace, December 2006, pg. 14. Al-Sadr's forces successfully infiltrated the national police and other security forces, often clashing with competing Shi'a factions operating within the Ministry of Interior. James Jones, *Report of the Independent Commission on the Security Forces of Iraq*, Center for Strategic and International Studies, September 6, 2007, pg. 88. Al-Sadr withdrew from Prime Minister al-Maliki's governing coalition in April 2007, although the Department of State continued to report that during 2007 "[p]articularly in the central and southern parts of the country, Shi'a militias—the JAM [Mahdi Army] and the Badr Organization —used their positions in the ISF to pursue sectarian agendas." "Iraq," *Country Reports on Human Rights Practices 2007*, U.S. State Department, March 2008.

[123] According to the Jones Commission, Islamic Supreme Council of Iraq (ISCI) member and former Iraqi Interior Minister Bayan Jabr "gave key ministry posts to members of the Badr Brigade, and Badr Brigade militia infiltrated police units in many areas of the country." James Jones, *Report of the Independent Commission on the Security Forces of Iraq*, Center for Strategic & International Studies, September 6, 2007, pg. 88. Even more troubling, Jabr created "Special Police Commando units composed of fighters loyal to Shiite militia organizations"—units that were later found to be "engaged in sectarian violence and death squad activities." Robert M. Perito, *Reforming the Iraqi Interior Ministry, Police, and Facilities Protection Service*, U.S. Institute of Peace, February 2007. The al-Maliki

government reassigned Jabr to the Finance Ministry in May 2006, following criticism from the U.S. government over militia infiltration and human rights abuses perpetrated against Sunnis by Ministry of Interior-linked death squads, although the U.S. Institute of Peace later reported that provincial police chiefs continue to "receive funds directly from the Finance Ministry for operations and salaries, [and] Baghdad has no ability to verify the accuracy of provincial budgets or account for how the money is utilized." Robert M. Perito, *Reforming the Iraqi Interior Ministry, Police, and Facilities Protection Service*, U.S. Institute of Peace, February 2007.

[124] "Iraq," *International Religious Freedom Report 2008*, U.S. State Department, September 2008.

[125] James Jones, *Report of the Independent Commission on the Security Forces of Iraq*, Center for Strategic and International Studies, September 6, 2007.

[126] Robert M. Perito, *Iraq's Interior Ministry: Frustrating Reform*, U.S. Institute of Peace, May 2008.

[127] Karen DeYoung, "U.S. Embassy Cites Progress in Iraq," *Washington Post*, July 2, 2008, A8.

[128] *Securing, Stabilizing, and Rebuilding Iraq: Progress Report: Some Gains Made, Updated Strategy Needed*, U.S. Government Accountability Office, June 23, 2008, pg. 29-30.

[129] Richard Tomkins, "Iraq: U.S. Troops Target Errant Iraqi Police," *RFE/RL*, April 18, 2008.

[130] Charles Levinson, "Iraqi Army Prepares to Pay Sunni Fighter Groups," *USA Today*, November 10, 2008.

[131] *Measuring Stability and Security in Iraq*, U.S. Department of Defense, September 26, 2008, pg. iv.

[132] *Human Rights Reports, 1 April – 30 June, 2007*, UN Assistance Mission for Iraq, October 2007, pg. 22.

[133] Ibid., pg. 23.

[134] *Human Rights Report, 1 July – 31 December 2007,* UN Assistance Mission for Iraq, March 2008, pg. 2-3.

[135] "Iraq," *Country Reports on Human Rights Practices 2007,* U.S. Department of State, March 2008.

[136] "Iraq," *International Religious Freedom Report 2008,* U.S. Department of State, September 2008.

[137] Transcript: "Prime Minister Nuri al-Maliki on Iraq," *CNN*, April 7, 2008.

[138] Hamid Ahmed, "Iraqi PM Freezes Militia Raids," *Time*, April 4, 2008.

[139] In August 2008, al-Sadr indefinitely extended the cease fire that he had imposed on his Mahdi Army militia in August 2007 and announced that the militia would be converted into a cultural organization, although his statement reserved the right to take up arms again depending on the result of the negotiations over the future U.S. troop presence in Iraq.

[140] "Iraq Fires 1,300 for Deserting Basra Fight," *Dallas Morning News*, April 14, 2008.

[141] Michael R. Gordon, "Al-Maliki's Basra move took U.S. off-guard," *The New York Times*, April 3, 2008.; Juan Cole, "Why Al-Maliki Attacked Basra," *Salon.com*, April 1, 2008; Dominic Evans, "Analysis: Maliki's Basra crackdown poses risks for U.S.," *Reuters*, March 29, 2008.

[142] Amit Paley and Zaid Sabah, "Case is Dropped Against Shiites in Sunni Deaths," *The Washington Post*, March 4, 2008, A12.

[143] "US Military Frees 2 Former Iraqi Officials After Court Drops Kidnapping, Murder Charges," *Associated Press*, March 5, 2008.

[144] It is not clear whether the perpetrators of this attack were Sunni Arabs or Sunni Turkomen. If the latter, this particular incident could mark the first sign of organized sectarian violence within Iraq's Turkomen minority community, which has both Sunni and Shi'a elements.

[145] Amnesty International, "Iraq," *Amnesty International Report 2007*, 2007.

[146] "Iraqi women fear going public as candidate," *Associated Press*, October 6, 2008.

[147] "Number of girls attending school dropping, say analysts," *IRIN News,* October 29, 2007.

[148] "Minister leads call to end violence against women," *IRIN News,* March 10, 2008.

[149] "Extremists fuel anti-women violence in Basra," *IRIN News,* November 20, 2007.

[150] "Women Forced to Give up Their Jobs, Marriages," *IRIN News*, May 30, 2007.

[151] Meeting with KRG Minister of Human Rights Yousif Mohammed Aziz in Erbil, Iraq, March 12, 2008.

[152] "Minister leads call to end violence against women" *IRIN News* March 10, 2008.

[153] Ibid.

[154] *Human Rights Report, 1 April – 30 June 2007*, UN Assistance Mission for Iraq, October 2007, pg. 14.

[155] *Human Rights Report, 1 January – 30 June 2008*, UN Assistance Mission in Iraq, December 2008, pg. 15-16.

[156] Statement by Special Rapporteur on Violence Against Women, November 25, 2008.

[157] "KRG establishes mechanisms to enforce laws protecting women from violence," *Iraq News*, May 14, 2008

[158] *Human Rights Report, 1 January – 30 June 2008*, UN Assistance Mission in Iraq, December 2008, pg. 16.

[159] *Human Rights Report, 1 July- 31 December 2007*, UN Assistance Mission for Iraq, pg. 16.

[160] "Kurdistan Parliament Forbids Forced Marriages" AlertNet.org, November 7, 2008.

[161] "Iraq's Kurdish areas prepare to ban female circumcision" *Agence France Presse,* November 22, 2008.

[162] "KRG to launch campaign to promote equality and end violence against women" Kurdistan Regional Government, November 16, 2008.

[163] "Iraq," *Country Reports on Human Rights Practices,* 2006, U.S. Department of State, March 2007.

[164] Interviews with Iraqi Christian refuges in Amman, Jordan on March 10, 2008.

[165] *Human Rights Report, 1 January – 30 June 2008*, UN Assistance Mission in Iraq, December 2008, pg. 15.

[166] *The Status of Women in Iraq Update to the Assessment of Iraq's De Jure and De Facto Compliance with International Legal Standards* (Washington, DC: American Bar Association, 2007), pg. 178-179.

[167] To protect academics, the Iraqi government provided university professors with a grant to hire private bodyguards and the offering of life insurance. Roadblocks were erected at campus entrances where security checks could be performed.

[168] *Human Rights Report, 1 January – 31 March 2007*, UN Assistance Mission in Iraq, April 2007, pg. 8.

[169] Ibid.

[170] Basim Al-Shara'a, "Baghdad Gays Fear for Their Lives," Institute for War and Peace Reporting, November 1, 2006.

[171] *Human Rights Regort, 1 November – 31 December 2006*, UN Assistance Mission in Iraq, January 2007, p. 26.

[172] Lou Chibbaro, "State Dept. 'troubled' over anti-gay violence in Iraq," *The Washington Blade,* May 25, 2006.

[173] Molly Hennessey-Fiske, "For Gays in Iraq, a Life of Constant Fear," *The Los Angeles Times*, August 4, 2007.

[174] "Iraq Displacement and Return, 2008 Mid-Year Review" International Organization for Migration, July 2008, pg. 1.

[175] There are currently thought to be 1.2 million Iraqi refugees in Syria, 450,000 – 500,000 in Jordan, 50,000 in Lebanon, 50,000 in Iran, 20,000 – 40,000 in Egypt, 10,000 in Turkey, and 200,000 in various Persian Gulf states. These numbers are estimates only. It continues to be very difficult for the UN Refugee Agency or the host nations to accurately tally the number of Iraqis residing in the country. The urban nature of the refugee crisis is atypical of most refugee situations where refugees live in camps and can be easily counted.

[176] Registration with UNHCR is voluntary and is often of interest mainly to those refugees who wish to be resettled to a third country. As of September 2008, UNHCR had registered a little moer than 303,000 Iraqi refugees throughout the region (active cases only), including 221,506 in Syria and 54,411 in Jordan. "UNHCR Statistical Report on registered Iraqis in Syria, Jordan, Lebanon, Turkey, and Egypt," UNHCR, September 25, 2008.

[177] UNHCR Situation Update, August 2008.

[178] Ibid.

[179] Ibid.

[180] "Iraq Displacement and Return, 2008 Mid-Year Review" International Organization for Migration, July 2008, pg. 2.

[181] Meeting with IOM Iraq, March 10, 2008.

[182] "IOM Emergency Needs Assessments, Post February 2006 Displacement in Iraq, 1 November, 2008 Monthly Report" International Organization for Migration, November 1, 2008, pg. 1.

[183] Interviews with Iraqi Christian refugees in Sodertalje, Sweden on November 12, 2007, in Amman, Jordan on March 8 and 10, 2008, and in Erbil, Iraq on March 12, 2008.

[184] Interviews with Iraqi Muslim refugees in Jordan, March 10, 2008 and in Syria, May 21, 2008.

[185] Interviews with Iraqi Muslim refugees in Syria, May 21, 2008.

[186] "Second IPSOS Survey on Iraqi Refugees, 31 October – 25 November", IPSOS, pg. 11. IPSOS is a market research agency contracted by UNHCR to undertake the survey.

[187] Ibid., pg. 12.

[188] Ibid., pg. 12.

[189] Meeting with IOM Iraq, March 10, 2008.

[190] "Survey on Iraq Refugees" Mercy Corps, March 2008.

[191] For example, in February 2007, Jordan began requiring all Iraqis entering Jordan to possess difficult to obtain G-series passports and prohibiting young men between the ages of 18 to 35 from entry. The government of Jordan views these restrictions as justified by security concerns in light of the bombings at three Western-owned hotels in Amman by Al-Qaeda in Iraq on November 9, 2005. Human Rights Watch reported in November 2006 that some Jordanian border patrol agents were turning away Iraqi Shi's, and to a lesser extent Christians, at the border.

[192] Interviews with Iraq Mandaean refugees in Amman, Jordan on March 6, 2008.

[193] Interviews with Iraqi Muslim refugees in Amman, Jordan on March 10, 2008.

[194] Meeting with UNHCR Jordan, November 19, 2007.

[195] Ashraf al-Khalidi, Sophia Hoffman, and Victor Tanner *Iraqi Refugees in the Syrian Arab Republic: A Field-Based Snapshot* The Brookings Institution—University of Bern Project on Internal Displacement, June 2007, pg. 14

[196] "Iraq Displacement and Return, 2008 Mid-Year Review," International Organization for Migration, July 2008, pg. 5.

[197] "Iraq Displacement and Return, 2007 Year in Review," International Organization for Migration, January 2008, pg. 5.

[198] "Iraq Displacement and Return, 2008 Mid-Year Review," International Organization for Migration, July 2008, pg. 5.

[199] "Iraq Displacement and Return, 2006 Year in Review," International Organization for Migration, January 2007, pg. 13.

[200] *Uprooted and Unstable: Meeting Urgent Humanitarian Needs in Iraq*, Refugees International, April 15, 2008, pg. 2 and pg. 6.

[201] "Parliament demands financial help for IDPs, refugees" *IRIN News*, September 25, 2008.

202 "Iraq Displacement and Return, 2007 Year in Review" International Organization for Migration, January 2008, pg. 1

[203] Ellen Knickmeyer, "An Iraqi Exodus, Out of Money and Options in Egypt, Some Refugees Are Heading Home" *Washington Post,* September 7, 2008.

[204] "Iraq Weekly Status Report" U.S. Department of State, October 1, 2008

[205] Under Saddam Hussein's rule, salaries per month for physicians were as low as $30.

[206] 45 Assyrian Families Return to Homes in Baghdad," *Assyrian International News Agency,* August 30, 2008.

[207] "Iraq Weekly Status Report" U.S. Department of State, December 3, 2008.

[208] "U.S. says Iraq should promote refugees' return," Reuters, June 3, 2008

[209] "IOM Emergency Needs Assessments, Post-February 2006 Displacement in Iraq, 1 October 2008 Monthly Report" International Organization for Migration, October 2008, pg.1.

[210] Ibid., pg. 1

[211] Testimony of Michel Gabaudan, UNHCR U.S. Regional Representative, to the Commission on Security and Cooperation in Europe (U.S. Helsinki Commission), April 10, 2008.

[212] "U.S. Humanitarian Assistance for Refugees and Internally Displaced Iraqis," U.S. Department of State, April 15, 2008

[213] Walter Pincus "U.S. to Admit 17,000 Iraqi Exiles, 5,000 More Refugees to Receive Special Visas Next Fiscal Year," *Washington Post,* September 13, 2008.

[214] This Act was an amendment sponsored by Senator Edward Kennedy (D-MA) to the FY 2008 National Defense Authorization Act.

[215] A P2 designation does not guarantee resettlement of all individuals from that category who apply. Each applicant still must undergo the refugee status determination interviews and background security and medical screenings required for all asylum-seekers by U.S. law. The P2 designation does, however, speed up the process for those applicants by bypassing the UNHCR referral process, and it also allows UNHCR to focus on other vulnerable groups.

[216] The relevant language is found in the following two sections:

Section 1243(a)(4): "Refugees of special humanitarian concern eligible for Priority 2 processing under the refugee resettlement priority system who may apply directly to the United States Admission Program shall include . . . Iraqis who are members of a religious or minority community, have been identified by the Secretary of State, or the designee of the Secretary, as a persecuted group, and have close family members (as described in section 201(b)(2)(A)(i) or 203(a) of the Immigration and Nationality Act (8 U.S.C. 1151(b)(2)(A)(i) and 1153(a))) in the United States."

Section 1243(b): "The Secretary of State, or the designee of the Secretary, is authorized to identify other Priority 2 groups of Iraqis, including vulnerable populations."

[217] Preeta D. Bansal and Nina Shea, "Iraq Must Avoid a Rollback of Rights," *The Washington Post*, August 4, 2005.

[218] Iraq Const. Art. 2(1).

[219] Ibid.

[220] Ibid., Art. 2(2).

[221] At that time, in dissent, Commissioners Bansal, Gaer, and Prodromou concluded that based on the severe human rights and religious freedom conditions extant in the country, and the sovereign government's complicity with, or toleration of, abuses as outlined in the Iraq chapter of the Commission's 2007 Annual Report, Iraq should have been recommended for designation as a country of particular concern (CPC), which is a categorization as set out in IRFA.

[222] Felice D. Gaer and Archbishop Charles J. Chaput, "Protecting Iraq's Religious Minorities," *The Washington Times*, December 22, 2006.

www.ingramcontent.com/pod-product-compliance
Lightning Source LLC
Chambersburg PA
CBHW080623290526
45790CB00007B/2899